KENDLERS'

KENDLERS'

The Story of a Pioneer
Alaska Juneau Dairy

By Mathilde Kendler

Library of Congress cataloging in publication data:
Kendler, Mathilde.
    Kendlers', the story of a pioneer Alaska Juneau
dairy.
    1. Kendler, Mathilde. 2. Kendler, Joe. d. 1967.
3. Alaska Dairy (Juneau, Alaska) — History. 4. Dairy
farmers — Alaska — Juneau — Biography. 5. Farm life —
Alaska — Juneau. 6. Juneau (Alaska) — Biography.
8. Juneau (Alaska) — History. I. Title.
SF229.7.K46A35 1984   636.2′142′0922 [B]   83-15684
ISBN 0-88240-255-2

Designer: Pamela Adams

Alaska Northwest Publishing Company
Box 4-EEE, Anchorage, Alaska 99509

Printed in U.S.A.

Contents

Foreword

It is difficult to maintain proper perspective as a publisher when the copy at hand deals with old friends and your hometown, and when the author of the moment used to serve you the nicest strawberry ice cream you ever lapped a lip to.

This is that kind of copy. Mathilde Kendler (nee Sauermann) was a 1922 immigrant girl from Germany to the United States. On the boat coming over she met Joe Kendler, an Alaskan dairy farmer from Douglas, Alaska, and a not-too-long-before immigrant himself from Austria who had been visiting the home sod. They fell in love. Some six months later (Mrs. Kendler insisted on the old-fashioned waiting period) the young German girl was on her way to Alaska, marriage, life on a growing dairy and the rearing of two fine children.

The story becomes also (it never ceased to be a love story) the story of a dairy that grew with the Gastineau Channel cities of Douglas and Juneau and thereby became an important sidebar in the histories of those communities.

That's all home country for this editor. We used to shoot ducks on the Kendler farm and adjoining Mendenhall Flats. Billy Mitchell and his squadron landed on a Kendler hay field. For years it was a dirt road of low standard that was a half-hour drive and is now a few minutes by freeway. Pan American bought a chunk of the farm for its first Electras connecting Juneau and Fairbanks, and now it is a modern jet airport. The Kendler farm is covered with asphalt and shopping centers, banks and gas stations.

Joe Kendler used to make his customer rounds daily to deliver his milk. Now Southeast Alaska communities and most other Alaskan cities get their milk from Seattle. The ads say it's good stuff, but it doesn't taste the same.

The Milk Man Comes No More.

An added note: When you find yourself ever delighted by the Kendler use of English studded with Germanisms you know that inevitably something will be lost in setting her words to type, but to totally "Englishize" her writing would be, if not sacrilege, at least destructive of a lot of this woman's storytelling charm.

At nearly 80, so happy she seemed ready to burst with it, she handed us the manuscript proudly noting, "It took I think, yes, 10 years. I didn't think I could ever do it!" Eyes twinkling, squirming with pride, she likewise emerged from her chrysalis as a struggling writer to let us know, authorlike, that autograph parties were already planned!

They should serve some of that wonderful strawberry ice cream we used to drive into the old Kendler farm for when Joe Kendler cut the salt marsh hay grass for his fat cows long before jetports and shopping centers.

Robert G. Henning

President,
Alaska Northwest Publishing Company

Preface

My husband Joe and I were lucky enough to have been part of Juneau from 1922 to 1965. We owned and operated the Alaska Dairy farm 10 miles out of the city for more than 35 years, and then we stayed on another 10 years after we gave up our business.

We knew many of the people of Juneau, both as friends and customers, and were active in the Alaska Pioneers, Eastern Star, the Masons and the Elks Club. I took part in the Juneau Women's Club, the Mendenhall Homemaker's Club and for over 10 years I was the leader for the Mendenhall 4-H Club for boys (and admirable boys they were — all 16 of them, of all ages!).

Several years in a row, with the help of the boys' parents and Joe, we entered floats in the Fourth of July parade, with all my 16 4-Hers happily riding in it. For three consecutive years we won first prize for the most original float — $600. That money was used to buy a stereo and educational records that all 4-Hers in the community could use; the purchase was made by Miss Charlotte Tomkins, the Extension Service agent.

In September 1965, after we had disposed of all our belongings in Juneau, Joe and I moved to a mobile trailer park in Washington State, where we found life very easy and enjoyable. We planted 18 colorful hybrid tea roses and 5 climbers that have grown enormously, exuding joy and pleasure for everyone. Joe died in 1967.

But my ties with Alaska have remained strong. Whenever I can, I return to Juneau. When I go back, I see the buildings of the Juneau airport standing on 75 upland acres that Joe cleared, plowed and seeded with domestic grasses for raising hay, and where our cattle grazed after the hay was cut. There is a supermarket now where our cattle run and barnyard used to be. And an extensive mall is where our lovely, two-story home and back yard used to

My hybrid roses planted outside my mobile home in Alderwood Manor give me great pleasure.

be. Our house has been moved a few miles farther north and is now the home of one of the children of Joe's business partner. That makes me very happy. All of Juneau's milk now comes from Washington State. That makes me very sad. Where our well-filled barn stood, there is now a very impressive-looking, busy bank with a drive-in window.

As I write, I still see the cattle grazing on that land in Juneau, I still see the hay barn filled to the high rafters with our own-produced hay. That used to make us so happy, especially when we got all the crop under shelter without a drop of rain on it. That always indicated speedy work of Joe and his men, and good managing methods on Joe's part.

I can still smell the appealing odor of our clean barn, taste the rich cream, butter and ice cream that came from our cows. And I remember it as though I were still a young woman, living and working there. I have written this book as I remember it.

—Mathilde Kendler

Acknowledgments

English is not my native language and I would like to thank Mrs. Ann Saling, who not only edited my many manuscripts, but also encouraged me to write this book. For more than 10 years she stood patiently by me. Her creative writing classes at Edmonds Community College in Washington State were most helpful.

I also want to thank Mrs. Mary Anne Mauermann for her expert help and encouragement.

About twenty-five years ago in Juneau, George Sundborg, an aide to then Alaska Governor Ernest Gruening, held a creative writing course. I knew then that we had a good story of our farm life, so I enrolled. I soon discovered what a steep mountain I would have to climb if I ever wanted to write our story. But George said, "Don't give up." So I plugged along. And finally it has happened. So now I want to say, "Thank you, George, for saying the right words that time."

And last, thanks to Jim and Bonnie Ramsey. Several times I had to call them on the phone. Jim's explanations were always helpful.

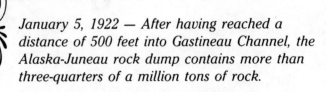

January 5, 1922 — After having reached a distance of 500 feet into Gastineau Channel, the Alaska-Juneau rock dump contains more than three-quarters of a million tons of rock.

March 1, 1922 — The Coast Guard Cutter Unalga, *Captain Brockaway commanding, has been assigned to duty in Alaskan waters with headquarters at Juneau. This is the first time in several years that a cutter has been assigned to Juneau.*

March 7, 1922 — Mike Pusich and Charles Miller have leased the Alaskan Hotel at Juneau for three years, according to James McCloskey, present manager and part owner of the property.

Chapter 1

America!

During World War I in Germany, the Allied embargo on food and raw material was so successful that food displays in grocery stores, bakeries and butcher shops completely disappeared. Potted geraniums were on display instead.

The war ended three years before I left for America, but wartime shortages were still just as acute. Factories stood idle, store shelves were empty. Looking at the store windows, I mentally stocked them with prewar goodies my grandmother used to make. Up in the attic, in her smokehouse that was attached to the house chimney (to conserve fuel during the meat-smoking process), I remembered her making spicy liver sausages and tasty head cheese, and cooking huge hams. Oh, how I'd love to inhale that wonderful fragrance again.

But during the war the smoke from the kitchen range and from the living room heater, going up the chimney, by-passed the smokehouse because it was empty.

And how I dreamed about my grandmother's large, out-of-doors baking oven, built of brick and mud. Once a month she baked from six to eight large, round loaves of dark pumpernickel bread, the size of medium wagon wheels. But first, before the bread loaves were pushed into the oven with a long-handled, wooden paddle, she baked several huge sheets of apple strudel, streusel and *kasekuchen* (cheesecake). Spellbound, I would watch her pull out the mouth-watering, golden-brown delicious treats. "Just wait a little until they are cooled off," she would tell me, "and I'll cut off a piece for you."

Men and time changed all this. White flour was no longer available. Hogs could no longer be fed. All those delightful delicacies became wartime casualties, leaving only precious memories to ponder.

I was one of the lucky people, able to escape the hopeless situation. An aunt of mine, living in Chicago, had sent me a boat ticket. I could work in her delicatessen.

The only regret I had in going away was leaving my loving grandmother. My mother had died when I was three, and my father had married again. And since my stepmother had children of her own, there was no special bond between us. So I lived with my wonderful grandmother.

On November 11, 1921, I boarded the SS *Hansa* in Hamburg. After the tumult and confusion of 500 passengers searching for luggage and staterooms had subsided, we all received our permanent placecards for the dining salon and an invitation to attend a get-acquainted assembly with coffee and cake that afternoon. At first the thought of walking in alone to meet all those strangers frightened me, but I summoned up my courage and went. There I saw the man who was to become my husband, sitting right across from me. Of medium height, with friendly, brown eyes, a pleasant, ruddy complexion, he looked strong and handsome.

Our eyes met and held. They seemed magnetized. He smiled and said, "My name is Joe Kendler. What's yours?"

Still looking into his eyes I stammered my name.

As he plied me with cake and cookies, I learned that he was returning from a vacation to his old home near Salzburg, German Austria, and that he was returning to Alaska where he owned a dairy farm.

As he spoke about his northern home, I listened in amazement. We had learned in school that Alaska was a land of ice and snow, and that no one could live there. Now I was learning it was a beautiful country. Though rugged, it was full of friendly people.

He must have been impressed and flattered by my enthusiastic attention, for he invited me to a deck dance and the movies that followed.

While I gladly accepted, I was bound that for me there would be no shipboard romance. "After all," I told myself, "Joe is a strange man, and I'm going to a strange land." So from the beginning I guarded myself against falling in love.

But in a few days that was exactly what had happened. And

I could see that Joe was becoming genuinely devoted. Although there were several other girls on board, he seemed to have eyes only for me.

One day Joe said, "Only three more days and we'll be in New York."

I began to feel unspeakably sad. I feared I would never see him again. I couldn't trust myself to say anything, so I kept silent. But he didn't say anything either.

Suddenly he asked, "Won't you come to Alaska with me? I love you very much. We could get married by the captain of this ship." Then he added, "If you say so, I'll go see the captain right away."

Tearfully, I explained, "Oh, I can't possibly do that. I can't marry right away. I can't let my aunt down, because she paid for my ticket."

"You won't have to worry about the ticket," Joe insisted. "I'll send her the money for it."

I also thought of an inherited tradition — a tradition binding engaged couples at least six months before getting married.

"But I can't let her think that I was so frivolous and rash as to marry the first man I met on this trip," I said firmly.

I assured him that I loved him dearly, but that I had to remain in Chicago for at least six months. Then we could get married. Joe accepted my decision. We both promised to write often.

"Die Dame der Amerikanischen Freiheit!" Joe explained as we passed the Statue of Liberty. The entire deck was crowded with people, all looking and admiring the harbor of New York. Ships flying flags of many nations were either docked or approaching. A small pilot boat on either side of our ship pushed us to port. A number of small launches cruised in the surrounding waters, as though to welcome us newcomers.

As Joe and I were standing at the rail talking, the ship docked. American citizens were requested to leave the boat first. So I bid Joe a sad farewell. Halfway down the gangplank he looked up to where I waved to him, and, lifting his hat German style, he called to me sadly, "Auf Wiedersehn." I watched him until he was out of sight. Then I turned my dazed gaze to my new homeland. The sight of the many skyscrapers gave me a momentary feeling of panic.

Suddenly I heard my name called over the loudspeaker. My name? Then it came again. I went to the purser's office, where I was introduced to Mr. and Mrs. Haller. Mrs. Haller grasped my hand warmly and said, "Your Aunt Kathe asked us to meet your boat and help you get through immigration." My papers were in order, so I could leave the boat immediately.

Since I had five hours to wait until my train would leave for Chicago, the Hallers took me sightseeing in their automobile. On our way through the dock area, I was flabbergasted to see men with large baskets hanging on their arms, filled with goodies, such as chocolate bars (I hadn't seen one in years), delicious-looking sandwiches neatly wrapped in waxed paper, oranges, and beautiful red apples polished to a high sheen. These men ambled among passengers waiting for transportation, offering the food for sale.

In wartime Germany no one offered anyone anything to eat. No one could spare it. Nor did anyone polish apples. In fact, a person was lucky to even have an apple to eat. He didn't care what it looked like.

Observing people on the street, I noticed they walked faster than in Germany and that their garments hung differently, draped more softly. Their clothes had more color, more style. I decided their fabric must be lighter weight and of a finer weave. I was also surprised to see men wearing gloves while at work. In Germany I'd never seen that either. Germany couldn't afford this luxury.

My hosts must have enjoyed seeing my eyes bulge and hearing my *Ohs*, particularly when they drove me slowly past a butcher shop. I fairly drooled at the rows of sausage, hams and bacon. Not since before the war had I seen such a display. It was like being in paradise!

Close by I saw another miracle — a bakery window with mouth-watering cream puffs, crunchy pecan tarts, and luscious-looking *kasekuchen* (cheesecake) on display. What a heavenly place! I thought.

Leaving these wonderful sights, the Hallers took me to a restaurant for a meal and then drove me to the depot and put me on the train for Chicago. I arrived there the following forenoon.

As the conductor helped me off the train, a little, short and chubby woman threw both arms around me. It was my Aunt Kathe. She held me tight, saying "I'm so glad you're here. Finally here." I was so touched by her warmth that tears came to my eyes.

I'll never forget the first meal she prepared for me in her apartment at the rear of her store. There was the most wonderful potato salad with lots of hard-boiled yellow eggs and mayonnaise, hard rolls, butter, pickles and a platter of scrumptious-looking sliced ham *with fat on it*! In Germany there was no fat on meat. Butchers removed it to sell it separately on the black market. Some people even thought that the fat had been used to manufacture ammunition.

Aunt Kathe took me to Marshall Field. Never, ever had I seen such magnificent displays. I almost went wild. In Germany, no one was allowed to touch the merchandise, only the clerk did that, holding it up for you to get a good view. But at Marshall Field, everybody picked up the merchandise. No one paid any attention. And such bargains!

I bought a pair of beautiful pajamas, blue with apricot trimming. Later I got another pair, apricot with blue trimming — each for just $1.25.

Chicago appealed to me more and more, particularly after I found my way around downtown. Now and then my aunt would send me to get something she needed. She would write out the number of the streetcar for me and where I needed to transfer. Away I would go with the greatest delight.

I could have been happy in Chicago, learning to restock shelves with groceries and serve customers. I had a cozy room and my aunt prepared wonderful food. But I missed Joe too much. I was thinking of him all the time.

November 17, 1922 — Four lights to mark the course across Mendenhall Bar have been installed with R.G. Keeney in charge of the work. The fuel containers for the lights hold enough to last eight days without replenishing. Pete Madsen is in charge of keeping the lights burning.

December 7, 1922 — The Alaska Electric Light & Power Company is now broadcasting programs by radio every evening from four until five and again from seven-thirty until nine. There are no broadcasts on Sundays. The programs consist of vocal and instrumental music and short talks, and the entire operation is in the nature of an experiment, according to W.S. Pullen, manager of the company.

Chapter 2

To Alaska

oe wrote often, and so did I. Every letter he finished with the message, "I'll be glad when you're here." But my six months wasn't up.

And then, for no apparent reason, I didn't hear from him any more. I took for granted that in case he found someone else, he would let me know. But, I thought, maybe he's sick, or had an accident. So I wrote two more letters. I felt sad, maybe I should have married him on the boat. Maybe he didn't like the idea of waiting six months.

About two weeks later I received a letter from Enumclaw, Washington. The sender's name was Anna Leirer.

"Who is she?" Aunt Kathe asked.

"I don't know," I said. "I never heard of her." Opening the letter, my hand started to tremble, and my aunt noticed. The letter was from Joe.

"What's wrong with you, why do you tremble like that?"

"Because I'm happy. I haven't heard from Joe for a long time." Then I noticed she had turned pale. In part Joe wrote, "I don't think you got my letters, because you never even answered one of many questions. Before you never missed any," he went on. "Do you suppose your aunt held back my mail to you?" He said that he had decided to send his letter for me to "Anna Leirer, the wife of my brother John's business partner in Enumclaw, and ask her to forward it."

Joe also said, "Your six months are up soon. Would you like for me to come to Chicago to help you get away? I surely would love for you to come."

Relieved that Joe still wanted to marry me, I started a letter

Joe's first cow barn on Douglas Island was this old, one-room schoolhouse to which he later added two lean-tos. On one side he stored hay and grain, and on the other he raised the calves. He could never find any official who would accept his rent money, so he used it for free.

to him at once, telling him that I could manage alone, and thanking him for the offer. I remembered that Joe had told me that the man he had engaged to replace him on the dairy while he went to Austria had sent him a telegram: "Come back home as quick as you can. The work on your dairy farm is too hard for me." So I feared that another trip so soon would be too great a sacrifice for Joe.

After Joe received my letter, he sent me a telegram, saying he would send me a ticket at once, and also telling me that agents would look after me on the way. I was getting really excited.

On various occasions my aunt told me that "a girl must be out of her mind to go to Alaska." She even stressed that "only rough men and drunkards go to Alaska."

No wonder she had withheld Joe's letters. She wanted to save me from disaster. Apparently my aunt had never heard anything good about Alaska. So I told her that Joe was neither rough nor a drunkard, but an appealing man.

On July 15, 1922, I left Chicago for Alaska. My aunt accompanied me to the train. As she kissed me good-by, she pressed an envelope into my hands, saying, "Take good care of this in case you need it for return ticket." After our wedding I was glad to be able to return the money to her from Alaska and to thank her for her warm-hearted guardianship.

As I entered the train and followed the porter, I was suddenly perplexed when I saw all the elegant luxury. Thinking I was in the wrong car, I immediately backed up to go out. But by the time I came to the door, there he was with my suitcase, saying, "Come with me, I'll show you your seat."

I was dumbfounded. Never in all my life had I seen such sumptuous splendor! All seats were upholstered with red plush; the very heavy carpet, too, was red. Each chair also had a white throw over the back. Joe must have sent me an expensive ticket.

In Germany, where average people make only short trips, trains are accommodated with wooden benches. There, Pullman-type luxuries are sought only by nobility or wealthy travelers.

I noticed in our Pullman how people spoke only in low tones, so that a comfortable, hushed atmosphere prevailed. But sociability was easy.

In Seattle, Joe's friend Anna Leirer met me at the train. Since I had two days to wait until the Alaska Steamship boat would leave for Juneau, Anna took me to their large dairy farm in Enumclaw. For me it was an unexpected pleasure to meet Joe's brother John, a business partner to Anna's husband. They all spoke German. So the visit was a pleasant interlude for me.

Two days later I left Seattle on the SS *Jefferson*. Leaving Puget Sound and Seattle was almost like closing a book. From now on my interests will have to be Alaska, I thought. Little did I know what all is entailed in becoming an Alaskan.

After we entered the Alaskan waters and I saw the wilderness along the shores, I felt uncomfortable. I was comparing the monotonous sight to the ever-changing scenery I had seen on the train. Every day I hoped we'd see open spaces.

In Germany all forests are cultivated, that is they are kept clean and clear of all underbrush, and not a dead twig is left lying on the ground. Forests there look like parks. So I had never seen wilderness, and I was not enough informed that this country is primarily wild. However, nothing would have deterred me from being with Joe.

I did enjoy some parts of the scenery, namely the hundreds and hundreds of little islands. But in my imagination, I chose the smallest ones, the ones I could easily use for a centerpiece and still have enough spaces for plates for guests at a dinner party. Perhaps

Joe on Prince; Douglas Island, 1919.

---

a few flowers stuck here and there, would surely be the talk of the party, I thought.

After three days and four nights I arrived in Juneau. As soon as the gangplank was in place, passengers started to disembark. When my turn came and I started down the plank, I saw Joe standing alongside of it so he could reach his hand up to mine, and so guide me down off the gangplank. His large, strong hand made me feel so secure.

After he greeted me, he began looking for my trunk and suitcase. "I'll have your trunk delivered to my place, but the suitcase we'll keep with you. Good friends of mine have offered me a room for you in their home for the time being." He added that they were German. We walked toward the ferry that would take us to Douglas Island, where Joe had his dairy.

At Douglas, then a small town of 700, Joe took me to the pleasant home of Mr. and Mrs. John Feusi, delightful people to meet, so warm and friendly.

"Let me show you to your room," Mrs. Feusi said, "in case you

Joe with his Arabian Prince hitched to the milk wagon he used to deliver milk in Douglas.

need to hang up some of your clothes." From the guest room, I could watch ships coming and going along Gastineau Channel.

Then Mrs. Feusi treated us to a delightful coffee and *kuchen* delicacy. "How are you making out with the house?" She asked Joe.

"Oh, I haven't told Mathilde yet. We were so busy talking about her trip," Then, to me, Joe said, "Tomorrow, after I finish with my milk delivery, you are to go with me to look at the house. I didn't want to close the deal until you saw it. The house is furnished and has two bedrooms."

The next day Joe and I walked through the house. I liked it at once, and Joe closed the deal. The seller's wife had died and he didn't want to live there alone. "That's the reason it's furnished," Joe said.

"Since Mr. and Mrs. Feusi have a hardware store here at Douglas, we might as well buy our dishes, tableware and cooking utensils at their store. And I'd like to turn that job over to you," he said smiling.

Every day I went to our new home to get things ready and to freshen all the drawers by washing them with soap and water and then letting them dry in the sun. The house was in good order and clean. I just wanted to make it more ours by giving it my personal touch. Every so often Joe would drop by and we had our arms around each other. It was so great to be together. I often thought about the narrow call we had had, almost losing each other. "Thanks to your good idea to send your letter to Anna Leirer in Enumclaw," I told Joe. "God wanted us to be together, because we fit together," I added. "Right you are," Joe agreed.

Our wedding on August 19, 1922, was small. Fifteen guests and my bridesmaid, Mamie, Mr. and Mrs. Feusi's daughter. She and I are good friends to this day. She and her husband still live in Juneau.

That same evening we spent in our own home, and remained there until Joe decided to buy Tom Knutson's homestead of 320 acres in Juneau. Later Joe bought 40 acres more. Our life was good and we felt the Lord's blessings.

July 19, 1923 — Joseph Kendler, owner of the
Douglas Dairy, yesterday purchased the dairy
business and ranch of Thomas Knutson. The
business is known as the Alaska Dairy. The
ranch consists of about 300 acres of land about
nine miles from town on the Glacier Highway.
Kendler will move his Douglas herd to the new
location, but will winter enough cows at Douglas
to take care of his milk customers there.

Chapter 3

We Move To Juneau

Three hundred and twenty acres! That's a lot of land. I wouldn't know what to do with it," I heard Joe exclaim. "How many cows do you have?" Mr. Knutson asked.

"Twelve."

"Twelve cows and not even a few feet of land to pasture them! That's some setup, and in Alaska where you must import every speck of grain and hay from Ellensburg, Washington, over a thousand miles away! Think of it!"

"I'm doing all right," Joe said. "I have paid up all my debts and have a few dollars in the bank."

"Joe, I don't doubt that you make ends meet, but you must consider that you work under a great handicap. In fact, for a dairy, yours is about the unhandiest setup I have ever seen."

"Well, Mr. Knutson, you must remember that opportunities are now limited here. Since the cave-in of the Treadwell Mine, Douglas Island is at a standstill. Many people are leaving because they can't find work here."

"This is just the reason I have come here to sell you my homestead on the Juneau side. There you could expand and develop."

I put lunch on the table. While we ate, Mr. Knutson talked more about his ranch. Suddenly he said, "Joe, don't you want to move, too, go where you have ample grass and feed for your animals, where you can go forward? You are a hard worker, you are young and able. What is holding you back?"

"We don't have that much money," Joe replied, with what I thought was a note of regret.

"If that's all that's bothering you, you needn't worry. I don't

We missed the ferry to Juneau from Douglas, so with Joe playing captain, we managed to get there in a rowboat!

want much money paid down, and I will make easy payment plans for you. Come over to Juneau tomorrow morning on the ten o'clock ferry and I'll show you the ranch."

We both anticipated the next morning with much enthusiasm and, as we retired that evening, we advanced the alarm clock by one hour for the next morning, so to be able to complete our chores in time to catch the ferry.

Mr. Knutson was on the dock, and right away we left on the drive along the highway. The gravel road ran alongside tideland and Gastineau Channel; on the other side was thickly forested hills and mountains. Joe and I were busy looking all directions so as not to miss any of the fascinating scenery.

Soon we arrived at the homestead. Joe seemed keenly interested, but I had lost my earlier enthusiasm, having by now become awed at the sight of those wide-open spaces.

"Three hundred and twenty acres surveys a half a mile square," said Mr. Knutson. "Let me show you the meadows with its tall grass, ready to cut and dry for hay."

Admidst the grass were large clusters of various wild flowers in beautiful colors. There were purple irises, pink lupines, shooting stars, yellow buttercups, goldenrods, violets and white daisies and more. We also found nice-looking red berries ripening close to the ground. Mr. Knutson said that they were nagoonberries, and grew all through the field.

"They are tart and have a pleasing flavor, and they make good-tasting jelly and wonderful nagoonberry pie. We also have lowbush cranberries and highbush cranberries on other parts of the ranch, as well as salmonberries and blueberries in our woods."

Finally we went through the barn, milk house and living house. The house had a large kitchen, pantry, large living room and one bedroom. No inside plumbing. That was a disappointment. The house was in good repair, but it needed painting inside and outside.

After we returned to Juneau and were dropped off at the ferry dock, we finally had a moment to ourselves to compare our impressions.

"Well, what do you think of it?" Joe asked.

"I can't say anything except that I am a little scared of it," I replied. "It looks terribly huge to me. Besides I don't know enough about land to form a helpful opinion. What do you think of it? Any decision on the matter will have to be made by you, since you are the trained dairyman and understand everything about it, land included."

He said, "You see, our cows can feed on grass here in Douglas only at the good will of the townspeople. So far there are no lawnmowers in Douglas. So the people all ask to bring the animals to keep their lawns short. But as soon as that free grass feeding stops, we would have to feed imported alfalfa in the summertime, too. That would mean that our profit in the business would be almost wiped out, he concluded. "This is why I am a little interested in that ranch."

"Joe, you must feel free to absolutely decide the way you see things. I'll gladly go anywhere with you, and I'll be ready to help wherever I can. I merely mean that I have to depend upon you to make the decision in this case."

A few days later Mr. Knutson came back to close the purchase agreement for the ranch. Our attorney then took care of the legal document.

Joe could hardly wait to buy himself a truck and get out to the place to start cutting down the ripe grass for his first hay crop on our own land.

But first we had to move the cows. To familiarize himself on the rough terrain that our cows would have to face on moving day, Joe rode his horse, Prince, to Juneau. On his way back to Douglas, as he was crossing Mendenhall Bar, the widest part of Gastineau Channel, Joe saw the tide coming in and advancing quite rapidly. "But," he said later, "I didn't worry, because Prince could swim." However, not being familiar with the area, and with the tide covering the bay so completely, Joe didn't realize that he was guiding his horse toward a very steep bank. When Prince suddenly climbed the bank, "I slid off the horse and fell into the bay. But I had enough presence of mind to grab Prince's tail. And dutifully, he pulled me up onto dry land."

Not far from there Joe spotted a log cabin. An elderly prospector answered his knock. When he saw Joe's wet clothes, he called, "Come in, come in. You need a set of dry clothes."

When I heard Joe's story, I went out to the barn and gave Prince, our hero, an extra treat of sugar, saying, "Thank you, thank you." That accident could have been so tragic, because growing up in the Austrian Alps, Joe had not learned to swim.

 *November 24, 1924 — Fire early this morning destroyed the greenhouse and a large part of the stock of the Juneau Florist Company. The greenhouse was located on the Glacier Highway.*

Chapter 4

The Rudys

Our first visitors were our neighbors, Mr. and Mrs. Charlie Rudy. Mrs. Rudy was a full-blooded Indian, short of stature and heavy. Her face was broad with a flat nose. Her hair was coal black and her large, black eyes were beautiful and warm.

The Rudys talked about their roadhouse, and how the townspeople drove out to enjoy Mrs. Rudy's famous chicken dinners. "She raises and processes her own light Brahma flock, a breed known for its large size, plumpness and its meatiness. She bakes them to a brown delicacy in her wood-burning stove," Mr. Rudy explained.

Mr. Rudy, a Harvard graduate, had come to Alaska during the gold boom. He said, "In those early days in Juneau the only white women were dance-hall girls. All the other women Indians. One night I got drunk, and the next morning I woke up married."

Before they left, Mr. Rudy stressed to Joe, "If anything ever goes wrong down here, so that you need an extra hand, just holler, and I'll be right down."

Joe and I were impressed with our neighbors. As the years went by, we became staunch friends who stood by one another.

The Rudys and our mutual friend and neighbor, Andy Delgard, often came to dinner at our house. For Joe and me their old-time Alaskan tales were ever fascinating.

Mr. Rudy had also a way of keeping us in stitches with laughter with his wit and clowning, while never cracking a smile.

One day he said, "I always maintain that marriage should be a 50-50 proposition. Whenever a wife gets a $50 dress, the husband should get a 50¢ shirt."

Here I am on Prince II; early 1920s.

I thought Joe would never stop laughing, it hit his funny bone. These were some of the joy times we had. Later when our two children, Mildred and Joe Jr., got a little older, our fun increased, because we could include them. Mr. and Mrs. Rudy always insisted, "Bring the children." And how much Mrs. Rudy enjoyed dressing up her husband to play Santa Claus for them.

One day, in the middle of winter, a great inconvenience arose. Our gasoline water pump broke down, and since the part had to be shipped from Seattle, we were out of water for four days.

Even though Jordan Creek, which ran alongside our yard, was frozen solid, in normal times we would have chopped holes and let the cows drink all the water they needed. But this time our yard was one huge sheet of ice, and cows can't stand up on ice.

"So," Joe said. "We'll have to bring the water to the cows in the barn." He hitched our team to the bobsled and loaded it with several 10-gallon milk cans. Luckily, the team had been sharp-shod. The two milkers filled the cans in the creek, and Joe poured the water along concrete troughs in the barn.

"When everything goes smooth and normal," Joe said, "you

pay no attention how much water a cow drinks. But when bringing it to her like this, it's a different story."

All 46 cows had to be watered like this. And the poor horses, how they had to pull that heavy load to the barn.

In the midst of all, Charlie Rudy drove up in his truck. "I just heard about your troubles. Here I am to give you a hand." Such a friend!

I was pregnant with our daughter, Mildred, and as my confinement drew nearer, Joe said, "We'll have to look around town to find a place for you to stay until the baby comes. Out here you're by yourself too long during the day. I worry about you while I'm in town delivering milk."

I didn't like the idea of having to stay in town with people I didn't know, especially in my condition.

Then Mrs. Rudy came up with a good idea. She said, "Charlie, you fix up that broken-down telephone line between our house and the Kendlers', then I can look after Mrs. Kendler while her husband is away."

After the phones were working, she called me every day to make sure I was all right. When she called on December 2, she asked, "What are you doing?"

"I have cleaned the kitchen stove and stovepipe," I told her. "I mopped the kitchen floor, baked bread, and now I have a cake in the oven." Suddenly I realized I had done an unusual amount of work.

"This is the day," she said. "Get ready. We'll be right down to take you to the hospital."

In no time at all they arrived in their panel truck. My suitcase had been packed for several weeks. Mr. Rudy carried it out and Mrs. Rudy helped me by hanging on to my arm.

In their covered truck Mrs. Rudy bedded me down on a mattress she had encased with a clean, white blanket, and covered me with a soft, luxuriously lightweight otter robe. When I referred to its rare beauty, Mr. Rudy explained: "The robe was a potlatch gift from her father, an Indian chief of a Southeastern Alaskan Indian tribe."

During the first night our sweet little girl was born. We named her Mildred Elisabeth. Immediately, when for the first time I held this precious bundle of joy in my arms, I sensed that an overpowering importance was added to my life.

Joe, too, smiled big as he rushed into my hospital room the next day.

"We are now three Kendlers," I greeted him.

In the meantime the Rudys' roadhouse became ever more popular. But there were rumors (and one day Mr. Rudy himself told us) that he was serving alcoholic beverages to their guests. That, of course, was against the law then.

One day, while a large dinner party was in progress, Mrs. Rudy went to the porch outside of the kitchen and left the door unlocked. Nearby were the enforcement agents, hiding and waiting for such an opportunity. When one of the doors was unlocked, they jumped up the steps to enter the house in great speed. Evidence was clearly at hand. All the guests were enjoying their alcoholic beverages, and Mr. Rudy was arrested. He had to spend one year in jail.

But that wasn't all the trouble. The other bad part was that the roadhouse, which was where they lived, had to be locked up for one year also. Mrs. Rudy did not want to leave. She decided to remain there to look after things. Before entering jail, Mr. Rudy put up a tent for her in their back yard. She tried hard to make the best of it, but one night, after several months into her tent, Mrs. Rudy walked the two miles down to our place. She said, "I'm cold and afraid."

At once I made coffee, then I bedded her on our living room couch, where she fell asleep almost right away.

The next morning we asked her if she would like to stay with us during the oncoming winter. Staying in a tent would have been almost impossible, during zero and sub-zero weather. Again she said, "I have to stay at home so that I can look after the place while my husband is away."

What could we do for her? Finally a thought came to me. "Mrs. Rudy, I would like to take you to the minister of the Native church in Juneau. My husband thinks that this minister could petition the proper authorities so that you could use your home during the winter."

The minister, who was also a Tlingit Indian, talked with Mrs. Rudy in their dialect. When they had finished, he told me that such a petition would have to go through the court. "I know the judge, and I know Mrs. Rudy's predicament, so that I can explain to him. I'll get busy on it right away."

A few days later a policeman brought Mrs. Rudy the key to her home. She was so happy. And we were relieved for her and her husband, too!

Joe often visited Mr. Rudy in jail after his milk delivery. Mr. Rudy always mentioned that he wanted his wife to move to town for the winter to be more comfortable. She would have none of that. She always insisted that she wanted to stay and guard their home.

Mrs. Rudy never complained about their misfortune, nor did she ever blame her husband for having sold liquor and putting them into those difficulties. Usually she kept herself busy, hunting and fishing. In both these sports she was as good as a man. She even killed a black bear, skinned it, cut it up for meat and hung up the meat to freeze.

When she cooked the bear chops, she wanted me to taste them, but I could not swallow more than one bite, much as I tried. The meat is too sweet for my taste.

Meanwhile, Mr. Rudy sent for government pamphlets to study the business of raising fur-bearing animals in captivity. As soon as he was released from jail, he started building long rows of wire pens and stocked them with mink and blue, silver and red foxes. In no time their business thrived.

One day, a few years after they began their fur farm, Mrs. Rudy brought me the most beautiful pelt of a crossbred red and silver fox all ready to wear. I still have it. She also brought a beautiful silver fox, ready to wear, for Mildred.

One year Mr. Rudy had to enter the hospital. A short time later he passed away. A few years after that, Mrs. Rudy, too, died.

Without our good friends, Joe and I never felt the same.

July 18, 1925 — The Goldstein Fur Farm,
11 miles from Juneau in the Mendenhall Valley,
is being enlarged, according to Charles Goldstein.
A new section is being built especially for
marten. The farm now has 9 pairs of silver
foxes, 30 pairs of blue foxes, 50 pairs of mink
and 16 pairs of marten.

Chapter 5

The Stranger

O ne evening as I was preparing dinner, I had just turned my stuffed pork chops to brown on the other side when I heard a gentle knock at the door.

I opened it and there stood a handsome young man of medium height with lots of dark, curly hair. His brown eyes were almost pleading as he asked, "Ma'am, would you have something to eat? I've come a long way, and I'm terribly hungry."

"Can you stay for supper?" I asked. "It'll be ready in another hour."

"No, I can't stay. I've a long walk ahead of me. But I'll be thankful for a sandwich."

He didn't offer any explanation of where he was headed, nor where he had come from. How unusual I thought! A man begging for food in Alaska, where at that time every able-bodied man could find work. He must be broke, I guessed, or he would have brought some food along for his long hike out in the country. I knew he needed more than a sandwich. My heart went out to him.

So I got busy heating up my tasty vegetable soup left over from lunch. I had prepared it from our own beef. I dished out the soup and made two thick sandwiches with beef, lettuce and sweet relish. He gulped his food so fast that I realized he must have been half starved. I refilled the soup plate and made two more sandwiches. All the time he ate, he didn't say a word, but watched me. At intervals I watched him, wondering where he was headed. Maybe to Eagle River. Then, it was the farthest settlement out the highway, about eighteen miles from our house.

I offered him a piece of apple pie. "No, thanks," he said. "I can't eat any more. But can I take it with me?"

With friends in front of our old house, 1928. From left, Dick Smith, Joe, Joe Jr., me, Mildred, Elizabeth Feusi, Mrs. Ralph Beistline and Joe Feusi.

As he was ready to leave, he asked, "Ma'am, could you spare a loaf of bread?"

"Yes," I said. "I'll get a paper bag for it."

In addition to the bread I also put in a second piece of apple pie and wrapped up several slices of roast beef. Reaching for the bag, he thanked me and walked out into the dark evening.

Feeling glad that I could spare him from hunger for at least a couple of days, I went back to my work and put him out of my mind.

As I added my finishing touches to my dinner, my thoughts went to my grandmother in Germany. Men begging for food had often come to her house. She never refused them. She usually had a soup on hand for such occasions. After she had answered the knock on her door, she would tell the beggar, "Just wait a minute. I'll be right back."

But the stranger always had to wait outside, because she would have closed the door on him and pushed the lever so that he couldn't open it. She would get busy heating up the soup and pouring it into a bowl. She would cut off a piece of her own black bread and would give it and the soup to the fellow, pointing to the bench in the yard where he could sit down to eat. If it rained, the beggar could sit inside an open shed.

However, these men, *handwerksburschen* (journeymen), were not regular beggars, they were young men who had served their master craftsmen's license, but they were also compelled to travel on foot for a full year and work for two weeks at a time for masters in many different sections throughout Germany. Their pay was small, so they depended upon people to give them some of their meals. I hadn't thought about this for many long years.

Later when the men came in for supper, I told Joe about the hungry man. "He surely looked sad and worried," I added. Meanwhile I got busy putting food on the table, and the subject of the unhappy visitor was quickly dismissed.

The following day when Joe came home, he brought an alarming report. "The whole town is in an uproar. They're all scared because a murderer escaped from jail two nights ago."

"Oh my word!" I became horrified. "Do you suppose . . . ?"

"It was," Joe nodded. "I told the chief deputy that it must have been the escaped convict who had come to our place for food."

I remembered his face, so sad and worried. But to have had a murderer in our house! To think by inviting him in I had exposed our two little children and me to such grave danger!

When Joe said that several posses were out searching for the man, I began to fear that he might return here, demanding shelter from me. I worried constantly because most of the time I was alone in the house with little Mildred, who was just two, and the baby, Joe Jr.

Then one day Joe came back from town and told me, "They've found him. They got him just as he was going to steal a boat at Eagle River."

What a relief! A week later he was taken to the penitentiary at Walla Walla, Washington.

But still those sad eyes haunted me.

January 28, 1925 — Some of the worst winter weather in many years is being reported by steamers and mail boats. The Estebeth, *on her last trip to Sitka, had to anchor in Tee Harbor for three days before she could get around Point Retreat.*

January 28, 1925 — The City of Juneau has just purchased its first combination grader and snowplow through Juneau Motors. The machine is identical to the one being used by the Bureau of Public Roads in keeping the Glacier Highway open during heavy snows this winter.

Chapter 6

Winters Don't Last

"I'm stuck," Joe said as he came to the house for breakfast. "There is just too much snow on the ground for the milk truck."

Though I tried to keep it from him, I knew I looked worried. But I wanted to be as brave as he in facing the inconveniences of wilderness living.

"Do you mean you have to use the horses to get the milk to town?" I asked.

"Yes, there is absolutely no other way. But always remember, winters just don't last," he added encouragingly.

Every day, the milk was bottled and placed inside wooden cases which were then stacked on the flat bed of Joe's long bob-sled and pulled by Nellie and Queen, our two, much-loved Belgian mares. They were obedient, never hesitating at any heavy pull. And that sled was heavy.

Joe usually left at six in the morning, dressed in a heavy mackinaw and a navy-blue striped stocking cap I had knitted for him with mittens to match. In one hand he carried the coal-oil lantern, and with the other hand, he guided the horses, returning home around four o'clock in the afternoon.

What bothered me most was that Joe refused my urging that he jump on the sled now and then to get some rest from the long trek through deep, soft snow in hip boots — the full 10 miles.

"No sir, I'm not going to jump on that sled," he told me. "The horses have all the pull they can manage without me on it, too."

One day I was startled when I saw Joe coming home around noon, the horses pulling the empty sled. *Ach, himmlischer Vater!* Empty! What could have happened? I waited anxiously until Joe had the horses unharnessed and comfortably bedded down in the stable.

As he walked toward the house, I opened the kitchen door, "What's wrong? Your sled is empty."

"Oh, yes," Joe replied in surprisingly good spirits. "This was a tough old day, one I'll never forget. But it could have been worse — I might have come home today without the horses."

I didn't know what he meant, but then he went on to explain.

"I parked my horses along the same corner of Calhoun Avenue as it meets Fourth Avenue, the way I've always done. But when I came back from my delivery at the Governor's Mansion and the entire neighborhood, the horses and sled were gone!

"Gone?" I echoed.

"Then I saw them galloping at high speed along Fourth Avenue, tails straight, manes flying, milk bottles and cases flying off both sides of the street. Me chasing after them. As I hung onto my two milk baskets with one hand and the other hand hanging on to my hat, I heard a fellow yelling to me from the other side of the street, "Hey, Joe, Mrs. Olson opened her umbrella, and they took off."

I could just picture the awful situation.

Meantime, the horses galloped down Seward Street and onto Main Street. "Luckily," Joe said, "I'd hung their snow bells around their neck, or they might have killed somebody."

From Main Street they had turned onto Marine Way.

"When I reached Marine Way, they were running at high speed toward the bay, and were already on the dock. I surmised that they could never stop themselves, and with their heavy harnesses and the heavy sled I knew they'd drown.

"And just as I thought this is the last time I'll see them alive," Joe went on, "I saw them make a sharp turn away from the bay and hit right smack into the dock building."

Luckily the tongue of the sled extended in front a good half-foot away from the horses, Joe said, so it took the greatest impact in that head-on collision, making a deep hole in the wooden building. The horses seemed stunned. But at least they were alive, even though they were trembling like leaves.

"But after I talked to them and patted them, they seemed to return to normal," Joe explained. "But I just couldn't take a chance

Joe with Nellie and Queen, our two work horses. Queen presented Joe with an unexpected colt one spring. It was quite a surprise, but it all worked out well.

on going up to town with them to pick up my bottles. I'll do it tomorrow, instead. We have enough bottles and milk cases in storage anyway."

The next day when Joe came back from town, he told me a heartwarming story.

"After I completed my delivery, I started looking for my lost supply of bottles buried in the snow. But no matter where I looked, I saw someone had gotten ahead of me. There wasn't a sign of anything left, but lots of marks of someone digging in the snow. As I came near the Goldstein Building on Seward Street, I found all my milk cases and bottles stacked in a neat row, ready for me to load up. It was then that I learned it was Mr. Olson, the husband of the woman whose umbrella started it all for me. "A wonderful ending," Joe mused.

Joe and the horses continued their rounds, but I felt sorry for them. So, I prayed for rain.

But instead of rain, Providence sent us something else. One day Joe came home, beaming with great and electrifying news: "A snowplow is on its way out here. I passed it at half-point. You better prepare a hot meal for the crew, seven of them. They'll get here in about four hours, or so. Have lots of hot coffee on hand, too."

At that time there wasn't anyplace where they could get something to eat. So it was essential that we take care of them.

Finally they arrived. When they entered the porch, they stamped their feet and shook themselves to get rid of the snow. But the snow did not budge. It was frozen to their garments. And when I saw their faces, I was close to tears. Never had I seen such a pitiful sight. Icicles hung from their eyebrows and from their stocking caps. Their faces were blue and immobile. They couldn't even talk at first, just sigh and groan and moan.

Joe kept refilling their coffee cups and I replenished their plates with spaghetti, my specially prepared sauce and meatballs and cole slaw. For their dessert I served them cherry pie with whipped cream. I knew they relished the food, but I also knew they hadn't eaten anything since breakfast, early that morning when they started out with the snowplow.

After they were thawed out, they told us how loose snow kept relentlessly flying over men and machines, killing and stalling engines and giving them endless troubles. The snowplow itself had no engine. Only a conglomeration of pipes and steel rods, a blade that pushed snow off the road and a high seat for the man to steer the equipment. That machine was being pulled by two caterpillar tractors and pushed by two others.

Even though that snow-removing model was a far cry from the modern machines of today, Joe and I liked the first model best.

May 12, 1926 — Paving Front Street with concrete from Seward Street to the Alaskan Hotel commenced yesterday. This is the first concrete paving in Juneau. The cost will be $10,000, including new sewer line under the paving.

Chapter 7

Wild Animals And Cows Don't Mix

Early one morning, a few years after we had arrived on our dairy, Joe came in for breakfast with a frightening story. "When I rode Prince out to the pasture this morning," he said, "I saw a strange animal among our herd. It was too dark to see clearly, but the outline was that of a pig."

"A pig!" I repeated, realizing that ours were in their pens.

"Well, it had about the same heavy neck and about the same height," Joe explained. "But when I rode up closer, I saw that it was a black bear!"

"A bear! What would a bear do to our cows?" I asked.

"I don't know," Joe said. "If they are hungry, you can never tell."

Oh, my, I thought. What a troublesome worry this could become!

The following winter proved to be horribly severe. There was from four to five feet of snow on the ground. A heavy blizzard kept us busy shoveling snow off the roofs and paths to the milk house and barn. Finally it stopped snowing and the sun came out. But it turned bitter cold. Luckily we had enough dry and chopped wood on hand to keep our house warm and the bunkhouse, too. On such cold days the snow-covered ground and every branch of trees and bushes sparkled like millions of crushed diamonds. I was looking out the kitchen window to admire winter's spectacular show, when my glance fell to our night pasture where Joe had turned out Queen and Nellie for a couple of hours of exercise. I enjoyed seeing them galloping around so happily, back and forth, with almost urgent speed. I went back to mixing my cake. Once I had it in the oven, I went back to the window to watch the horses again. Now I noticed

Nellie and Queen getting a special handout — sugar treats — from the kitchen window.

a dog with them, running right alongside them. Amused, I thought, how nice. Even a dog wants to play with them! Then, still watching, I began to realize they didn't seem all eager to play with the large dog. It seemed to me that they wanted to get away and were shaking their heads every time the animal jumped up toward them. Uneasy, I ran over to the barn to tell Joe about the strange animal.

Joe dropped everything and ran fast to the house to get his rifle. "That's a wolf!" he yelled over his shoulder. The wolf was too close to our horses to fire at, so Joe shot into the air. At once the hungry beast raced back to the woods. Queen and Nellie stuck very close to Joe as they walked back to the barn. On my way back to the house, a trembling shiver ran through me. A wolf! Oh, my dear God! So near the home! The night pasture was only 150 feet from the house! All through the evening meal the men talked of wild animals. Listening, I shuddered, wondering what to expect next.

That night I heard bone-chilling howls. It seemed that a whole pack of hungry wolves was crying their dismal wail of woe and hunger. Even after I pulled the blanket over my head, I couldn't shut out their pitiful howling.

"What's the matter?" Joe asked. We had heard wolves howl other nights, but it hadn't upset me like this. "Can't you sleep?"

"Not with this racket." I answered. "I'm afraid. I'm even afraid to go out to the woodshed tomorrow for firewood."

"Don't worry about that," Joe said. We'll fill the woodbox for you."

For several days after the horse episode, the men watched for wolf tracks in our yard. To my great relief they found none.

The following spring, when the grass was long enough to drive our cattle out to pasture, Joe made a heart-breaking discovery. He found one of our very fine, young heifers lying in the grass, dead. Her tongue had been torn out! Joe didn't think a wolf had done it. "He would have eaten more than just the tongue," he said. "This is the kill of a wolverine."

By now I feared that the killing would turn into an epidemic. In summer, when there is lots of pasture available, it is just too impractical and costly to keep the animals sheltered and fed inside the barn.

Joe had a better idea. One of our men, Herb, was an expert shot. With our rifle, Herb watched over our animals, hiding himself and lying in wait for the beast to return for another kill. And two days later, return it did. Herb came home, dragging a dead wolverine behind him. How happy and relieved we felt!

Apparently that was the only wolverine in the area, unless the others had left after the shooting. After that we never lost another animal.

August 4, 1926 — Publication of a magazine devoted to the geography, history and commerce of Alaska will start publication about August 25. It will be known as Alaska Magazine.

August 26, 1926 — The Auke Lake Loop bridge over the Mendenhall River will be opened to traffic on the 28th. The bridge was constructed by the U.S. Bureau of Public Roads.

Chapter 8

TB Disaster

Joe built up such a big clientele in Juneau for his milk, whipping cream and buttermilk that he ordered 11 Guernseys from Washington State, doubling our small herd. We were delighted with them. They arrived with shiny coats, lively eyes, and soon proved their worth, producing heavily, with excellent butterfat count. After the first winter, the state cattle inspector, Alaska's only veterinarian, arrived to make his annual tuberculosis tests on our cows. We were not concerned because our herd always had passed 100 percent.

Joe explained to me the mechanics of the test. The tuberculosis culture is injected into the softest spots under the cow's eyes and under the widest part of her tail. After three days, the veterinarian returns to examine them. If there is no reaction on the injected spots, the cow is safe. But if there is swelling, the test is positive and the animal has to be destroyed.

This time the veterinarian returned as usual and checked our cows. After he left, I looked out the window to see Joe walking slowly back toward the house, his head down, his shoulders sagging.

Apprehensively, I opened the door and asked, "Is something wrong?"

He nodded, "All the new cows . . ." he began, then swallowed hard. "I have to destroy them. The vet said the meat can be sold. But I won't expose my customers to tainted meat. I'd rather take the loss."

After the initial shock wore off, Joe hired extra helpers to dig deep trenches on our tideland acreage. The salt water would kill any living TB bacteria in the soil.

The men herded the cows close to the trenches, and Joe shot

one cow after another with his rifle, right in the center of the forehead. I couldn't bear to watch, but I heard the shots. Great quantities of lime was shoveled on top of the cows and the trenches were filled with earth.

Joe couldn't talk about it afterward. I felt indescribably sorry for him because he loved his animals, and sorry for the cows themselves. They died in their prime. But I held back my tears to make it easier for Joe.

We were so short of milk that we had to buy from other dairies to meet the demand. But Joe wanted to use only his own milk, so the next spring he decided to order another dozen cows.

"I need them," he insisted. "The first ones died because of our severe winter. The next ones I'll shelter during the cold weather." He was sure they would soon become acclimatized.

Again we ordered the cows, and again Joe was highly pleased with both their appearance and their production. We now had 34 animals and, for the time being, plenty of milk for all our customers' demands.

That fall, after harvesting our own hay crop off our meadows, Joe contracted a severe case of tonsillitis and had to enter the hospital. That very day the cattle inspector came to make his annual TB test. Remembering the terrible day a year earlier, I was uneasy while he worked in the barn, injecting the cattle.

Two days later, before he returned, I went into the barn to see for myself that everything was all right, so that I could tell Joe in the hospital.

I was horrified to see one of the dozen cows was swelling the size of large duck eggs around the injected areas. Numbly I moved through the barn, checking cow after cow. Each of the new cows had the same swellings.

How could we financially survive the loss of another dozen cows? How could Joe survive the emotional shock of destroying them? At the hospital I couldn't bring myself to tell him. Another day and he would be home, a little stronger, better able to bear the horrible news.

The following day he came home. Eagerly he changed to his work clothes at once and went out to the barn. When he came back into the house, a few minutes later, he looked grim.

"I already know," I said, to spare him the pain of telling me.

A big load of our very own hay. Joe liked to produce his own hay and it was more economical, too; importing hay from Eastern Washington was very expensive.

For a long time he sat in our kitchen, staring at the floor. Finally he said:

"I've sheltered those cows from the cold and wet ever since they arrived. They didn't get TB in our barn. They were reactors before they left Washington."

Late that afternoon the veterinarian came. He, too, was convinced that the cows had arrived in Juneau already carrying the bacteria.

We had to play the sad scene again, destroying apparently healthy animals. It was no easier the second time.

Our veterinarian got in touch with the veterinarian of the county in Washington where we had bought the herds, requesting information on Washington health laws. He learned that although there was a state law that no milk could be sold in Washington from TB-reactor cows, nothing was specified about not selling the live animals. So the law had not been violated. There was nothing we could do to recoup our loss.

The Alaskan veterinarian then went to the legislators and explained what had happened to us and the potential danger to all of Alaska. At the next session, the legislature quickly passed a law demanding a health certificate for every animal entering Alaska. Moreover, it reimbursed us for two-thirds of our losses from the tubercular cows we had had to destroy. I find it incredible now that lawmakers could act so quickly.

March 9, 1929 — Frank Maier and Tony Reiss have purchased an 88-acre tract near the Mendenhall River and will establish the Alaska Dairy.

May 27, 1929 — The Boy Scout cabin at Eagle River was virtually completed over the weekend by a crew of men and Scouts and everything will be ready for the start of the summer encampment starting next week.

May 31, 1929 — Dr. H. Vance and several associates have opened a flying school with Lyle C. Woods as instructor. The first flight was made today from the tide flats near the Alaska Dairy.

Chapter 9

Bourbon-Flavored Ice Cream

Even with the help from the legislature, it took a few years to recoup our losses from the tubercular cows. I thought a great deal about what I could do to help. I began to dream about making ice cream to sell to the townspeople, since we had most ingredients on hand at the farm. Occasionally, I made a small batch for dinner, and Joe and the hired help who ate with us always complimented me on how smooth and rich it was. Mildred and Joe Jr. loved to scrape the dasher.

One evening in late spring after the men had gone to the bunkhouse and we were alone, Joe told me with a worried frown, "We're getting too much milk again. It's the same every year at this time. All that tender, new grass increases our milk flow."

The time seemed right to mention my dream.

"Why can't I use the surplus milk and cream to make ice cream for sale? We could get 60¢ a quart, I'm sure."

"No!" was Joe's first reaction. "That would be too much work for you. You have enough to do, cooking for the men and taking care of the children."

But I couldn't be talked out of the chance to make some badly needed money.

"Just in the summertime," I said. "When we have too much milk. You or one of the men can help me crank the freezer."

Joe was quiet for a few minutes. He knew we needed the money and we had to get rid of the extra milk. Finally he said, "All right. Try it for a while. Ed can crank the freezer in the forenoon while I'm on the delivery truck. And, in the afternoon I can help you."

Ed, our handy man, was a good worker when he was sober.

Joe and me in the early 1930s.

He seldom got drunk on our place but he was well known in every bar in Juneau, especially on payday.

Two weeks later two new freezers arrived from Seattle. I felt already set up in business and earning money.

I placed an ad in the *Alaska Daily Empire*: "Homemade Ice Cream Now Available At Kendler's Alaska Dairy."

Early Sunday morning, with lots of rich, thick cream and milk and our own eggs on hand, I began making my dream a reality.

Out in the shed Ed was chopping ice while I made the custard and poured it into the two freezer cans. He carried them out to the shed and set them inside wooden tubs. As we added ice and rock salt, I explained the cranking process.

"You can't stop once you start," I warned him. "To get a smooth texture it is important to keep a steady rhythm and a medium speed. Call me as soon as it thickens."

Ed nodded. "I'll do everything just the way you said, Missus."

Happily I went back to my kitchen, intending to prepare lunch for the men early. If all went well, my ice cream customers would require my attention by noon.

Glancing out the window a few minutes later, I was appalled to see Ed hurrying to the house. What could have gone wrong? I opened the door and called out to him:

"Ed, you mustn't leave the freezer."

"I'll tell you something, Missus," he said, shaking his finger for emphasis as he came into the kitchen. "Cranking would go much easier if I could get a little drink."

"A drink!" I was flabbergasted. "I don't have a thing."

"Why don't you look around," he suggested slyly. "You might find something."

Suddenly I remembered that Joe kept a bottle of bourbon in the cupboard behind my mixing bowls. He used it so seldom that a bottle lasted him at least a year. Ed must have seen that bottle some time when I had had the cabinet door open. I felt cornered, knowing that Ed wouldn't crank until he got a drink. I had to save my ice cream.

Frantically, I pulled out the almost-full bottle and poured Ed a drink. With trembling hands, he reached for the glass, tilted it, and swallowed the whiskey in one gulp. Refueled, he rushed back to the shed. Soon I heard a steady cranking sound, and I went back to my lunch preparations.

In a few minutes he was back at the kitchen door.

"Just one more, Missus," he begged.

Worried about my ice cream and knowing that the customers would soon be coming in another hour or so, I poured Ed another drink.

The intervals of cranking became shorter and shorter. I had to pour Ed another drink, then another and another. Fighting tears, I begged Ed to keep on cranking. In desperation I ran out to crank the second freezer. By this time Ed didn't care if the ice cream froze or not.

When I saw a car driving through our white picket gate, my

emotions were mixed. I was delighted to see a customer but apprehensive over the delay, worried he might not want to wait. I would have to stall him off and hope the ice cream was good enough to sell when it was done.

I went out to explain to the man that we were a little late. Just then I saw another car approaching, and I asked him to pass the word on to anyone else who came.

Before long a whole caravan of cars was parked in our driveway, with the drivers no doubt amused by our high-gear activity. Little did they realize I was desperately trying to keep a drunken man busy at the crank.

At last the ice cream was ready. I feared the worst. Surely it would be awful.

I dismantled the crank and took off the top of the can and dug a spoon in the frozen cream. It was delicious! It even tasted slightly of bourbon, I thought.

Relieved, I sent the children out to the waiting cars to spread the word that the ice cream was ready while I scooped it out and packed it into quart cartons. I sold it right down to the last quart.

By the time Joe came home I was exhausted, but thrilled by my success. I had made almost $15.

Joe was pleased with my success.

"Not bad!" he said, patting me on the shoulder.

The following Monday I went into Juneau to shop for groceries. Afterward, I did something I had never before done in my entire life: I went into a liquor store. I replaced Joe's bottle and bought one for Ed. I had to prepare for the next cranking session.

January 1, 1930 — The Alaska-Juneau Gold Mining Company in 1929 had the best year so far recorded. Production was $3.5 million with an operating profit of $1.1 million. A total of 3,840,000 tons of ore were trammed out of the mine.

February 17, 1930 — Juneauites are digging out from three feet of snow that has fallen in the past three days. Auto traffic is limited to delivery trucks and few of them are running. The city snowplow has been kept busy and has kept most streets open except on Starr Hill and in the Seater Tract.

February 2, 1931 — The flag was raised for the first time over Alaska's new Capitol Building this morning by Governor George A. Parks, while 400 schoolchildren cheered. The event marked the occupancy of the $800,000 Federal and Territorial Building by government offices.

Chapter 10

Frontier Spirit

hortly after I arrived in Alaska, I began to hear about "frontier spirit." I had difficulty understanding the right meaning.

"What does it mean?" I asked Joe. "My German dictionary defines frontier as borderline land."

"Frontier spirit means helping others," Joe said. "Out here at Mendenhall Valley where there are only a handful of people, we depend on one another." He went on to say that whenever someone came here, whether in trouble, or just lonely, we should stand by him, helping or encouraging.

And many did come to us for help, more often in winter than in summer. They were mostly fishermen who had their own boats, but no land transportation, since there were no roads in their area. To shop for food and other things in summer, they took their boats to Juneau. But in winter they had to pull their boats out of the water, because sub-zero weather froze the shallow bay to thick, solid ice. Their boats would have been demolished at high tide when huge sheets of ice broke up and piled along water's edge.

So they had to walk to Juneau, a strenuous trip of 10 or 12 miles through difficult terrain at low tide, especially from Fritz Cove and from Fish Creek, on north Douglas Island. Even at low tide they had to wade through considerable water in the shallow part of Gastineau Channel.

From our farm we could see the small Fish Creek bachelor settlement not so much by their small, low-built, one-room cabins, but by their wood-burning smoke stacks that sent up streams of blue, curling smoke, especially during sub-zero weather. "It looks like the men over at Fish Creek keep busy and cozy," Joe said.

The first time I met one of them I had a demonstration of what Joe meant by frontier spirit. Early one morning, Joe and his helpers, seated around our breakfast table in the kitchen had just begun pouring thick cream onto their steaming-hot oatmeal when we heard heavy steps on our back porch. Since I couldn't leave my hot cake griddle just then, Joe got up to open the door.

"Howdy," I heard a friendly voice greet him. "Nelson is my name."

"Howdy yourself, Mr. Nelson. Come right inside. You're just in time for breakfast." Joe pulled out a chair for our visitor. "What brings you here so early in the morning?"

"Well, over there on the island me and my two neighbors are running low on staples. And when we heard you people bought the Tom Knutson homestead and started a milk route in Juneau, we thought that one of us should try to bum a ride with you. Do you mind?"

"Not at all, Mr. Nelson," Joe assured him. "Any time you or your neighbors need a ride to town, just come over here. You're welcome to ride with me any time. I leave at 6:30 every morning."

I placed a stack of hot cakes with fried eggs and crisp bacon before the men with an extra plate for Mr. Nelson. As they ate, he told how he and his friends supplied themselves with meat, game and fowl by hunting. They raised their own carrots and potatoes. "Each of us has salted down a small barrel of black cod. They are delicious! I can tell you," he emphasized. "They call me Snubnose Nelson," he said laughing. "And I call them Stovepipe Bill and Saltwater Mack."

Mr. Nelson and his two friends were only the first of many who needed our help. It was only a year later that I really came to understand what frontier spirit involved.

One summer forenoon, just as I was starting to prepare a hot lunch, I heard a knock on the kitchen door. Opening it, I saw a clean-cut young man of about twenty. Sensing that he needed help, I invited him in.

"No, thank you, Ma'am. I'm Carl Nielson. I'm in trouble and need help."

"What kind of trouble," I asked.

"Well, I bought a second-hand truck on Douglas Island. But I didn't have enough money to pay the Alaska Steamship Company

Joe Jr., 5, on Peanuts, our pet pony; 1930.

to freight my truck to Juneau. So I decided to drive it along the beach and across Gastineau Channel to the mainland at Mendenhall Valley and from there to Juneau. But I got stuck on this side in wet sand."

"Can you wait until the men come home?" I asked. He shook his head. "No Ma'am, I can't wait. The tide is coming in and it'll ruin my truck." I felt my heart go out to him, he looked so sad.

"I saw your dump truck in the garage," he went on. "I noticed its dual tires. It would pull my truck out easily, and it wouldn't take very long."

Oh, my, I thought. If only I knew where Joe had sent our helpers this morning to repair fences. But on 360 acres I couldn't start looking for them. How could I drive that clumsy dump truck on that uneven area. I decided quickly I'd better say I couldn't drive, or that I didn't have the key, or that the baby was going to wake up any minute. Then I looked at his sad face and I knew I just had to help.

Just then I saw our neighbor Andy Delgard strolling into our yard. Every morning he came to get the previous day's newspaper. Too bad Andy couldn't drive. "Would you mind staying a little while until I get back?" I asked him. "I have to help this man, but I'll be right back. The baby won't wake up before noon."

He nodded. "Sure, I stay."

Carl and I walked toward the garage, and somehow I got that heavy dump truck backed into our driveway and over our night pasture to the end of our land. It was rough going.

As we jolted along over the slimy and rough tide flats, I noticed heaps of brownish kelp and green seaweeds. I smelled their salty odor on the crisp morning. Countless sea gulls flew over the flats, diving and picking up mussels and clams. They would drop the shells on a pile of rocks near the water's edge and then dive down to pick up the morsel of meat. As we drove toward Carl's truck, he told me about his widowed mother and younger brother. "This truck will help me earn more money so that I can help them."

Suddenly about half a mile from our gate the Ford stopped. We came to an abrupt halt. I felt the left front wheel sagging and pulling downward. Puzzled, we got out to examine the situation: the trouble was serious — the left wheel was in quicksand. We tried to get the truck going again, but nothing helped.

Ach, Du guter Gott im Himmel! What had I done! There was Joe's expensive truck stuck on the tide flats. If it was destroyed by the tide coming in. . . . The next week our haying season would begin. Without the truck we might lose our crop. And all because I had tried to help a young man. Frontiers have limits, I thought with anguish.

Sadly, Carl hurried over to his truck to see if he could get it out. I ran back to the house, tears streaming down my face. The baby was still asleep, so I went back to preparing lunch, worried sick about Joe's truck.

In the meantime, Andy, who had been reading the newspaper in the living room, strolled into the kitchen. Surprised, he asked, "Why the tears?" After I told him what had happened to the truck, he said, "Don't worry, the tide won't be in for another two hours."

Not to worry is better said than done, I thought.

Looking out the kitchen window, I saw Joe coming home half an hour earlier than usual. Quickly I dashed over to the milk house.

He took one look at me and asked in alarm, "What's wrong? Why are you crying?"

Pointing toward the tide flats I stammered. "Your truck is stuck down there."

"My truck? What is my truck doing on the tide flats?" He was almost yelling, his brown eyes wide. I explained about Carl Nielson.

Suddenly he was all business. "Never mind," he said. "I'll go get the fellows to help me." Jumping on his milk truck, he left in a hurry. In no time he was back with our three hired men who had been repairing fences all morning.

Everybody began rushing around, loading timber, planks, heavy chains, ropes and truck jacks. Then down to the flats they went.

Encouraged, praying for their success, I set the table and added the finishing touches to lima beans that had been baking all morning with our own smoked pig hocks.

Finally I heard them drive into our yard. I rushed to the window and saw them drive the dump truck following the milk truck. I almost cried again in relief.

Joe was the first one who came into the house. He walked over to the stove where I was dishing up the beans and put his arms around me. He looked down at me with a smile, "Now you know what frontier spirit means! You tried, anyway!"

How about Carl's truck?" I asked Joe.

"Oh, he is already halfway to Juneau with it," he said.

After lunch, when the men left the house, I went outside, too. I stood watching the afternoon flood tide, it seemed to wash away my unhappiness of the morning ebb tide.

May 19, 1932 — The German cruiser Karlsruhe, *with a complement of 560 officers and men, is visiting Juneau for 11 days. The vessel is in command of Captain Erich Wassner and left Keil, Germany, last November.*

June 4, 1932 — The Juneau City Council last night voted to issue a warning to all steamship companies touching here that stowaways will not be allowed to land and that they will have to be returned to their ports of embarkation at the transportation company's expense.

August 25, 1932 — Juneau will be the only town in Alaska which will hold its annual fair this year. The Southeastern Alaska fair will open in the Juneau Fair Building on September 14 and will run for four days.

Chapter 11

Midnight Medicine

W hy park on such a dark street?" I asked Joe, after he drove past the ferry dock toward the dead end on Ferry Way.

"Well," he said, "this is where Dr. Richard (a pseudonym) asked me to wait for him. I guess he doesn't want anyone to find out what he's going to do."

While we waited for the ferry, I remembered how hesitant Joe had been about asking Dr. Richard for help. Joe had an emergency in our horse barn and needed a veterinarian. But the closest and only one was in Fairbanks. Joe was well aware that the Juneau physicians would be too busy with their patients to help us, but Dr. Richard was new in Douglas and needed the business. So, after a week of worrying, Joe had called on him.

"Dr. Richard, would you be willing to come to our dairy farm on the Glacier Highway to remove a tumor on the fetlock of Queen, my Belgian mare? There's no veterinarian in Juneau. The only one in Alaska is in Fairbanks."

Dr. Richard had looked startled and dubious.

Quickly Joe had explained. "The tumor is growing bigger every day. Queen is an exceptional horse, and I can't afford to lose her."

Dr. Richard had hesitated. "Mr. Kendler, I'm not a veterinarian. Still I realize your predicament, so I'll help you out. But you and your wife must not breathe a word about it. No one must hear about my operating on your horse."

Joe had understood perfectly. Dr. Richard did not want potential patients to think of him as a horse doctor. He then promised to come out the next evening.

Finally we heard the *Teddy*. Soon we saw a shadow alongside our car. Joe got out and greeted Dr. Richard, a tall, handsome man in a gray suit. He slid into the car.

Turning to me, Dr. Richard said, *"Wie gehts?"*

"Danke, ganz gut" (Thank you, I'm fine), I answered, expressing surprise at his excellent German accent.

"In my student years," he explained, "I spent two years at the Medical Institute in Heidelberg." Then, turning to Joe, he said, "I took the last ferry across to Juneau, so that there would be no one from Douglas to ask me questions. I'm spending the night at a friend's house in Juneau. I told them I had to make a sick call. Are we going directly to the farm?" he asked.

"Yes, we are," Joe said.

At the farm we went right to the cow barn.

The outside door of the horse barn was locked "to prevent the strong west wind from pushing the door open," Joe explained, that door being the only one facing west. Our various buildings — cow barn, calf barn, horse barn, feed barn and hay barn — were all combined in a large complex, separated only by inside walls and doors. For more convenience and also for better air circulation, Joe always kept the doors open. So it was easy to get from one section into another.

On our way through the cow barn, we noticed the cows were fast asleep. Not a sound could be heard. For just a moment Dr. Richard stopped at the open door of the hay barn. He breathed deeply. "Umm," he said. "It's been a long time. I'd forgotten how sweet grass hay smells."

Once in the horse barn, Dr. Richard took a quick look at Queen's swollen hind leg, spoke gently to her and then removed from his satchel a long, white rubber apron, which he put on.

Joe fastened a rope around one of Queen's front legs and around her good hind leg. Tugging gently, he caused Queen to drop slowly onto her front knees and then lie down onto a soft bed of new straw.

Dr. Richard patted the heavy, 16-hand-high black horse reassuringly, touching the white mark in the middle of her forehead. Deftly he gave her an injection in her neck. Soon Queen put her head down and closed her eyes. The operation began.

During the operation I played head nurse, running for hot water, soap and towels, gunny sacks, whatever they called for.

Our happy family: Mildred, 9, me and Joe, and Joe Jr., 8.

Once when I had to return to the house for an old towel, I put on a pot of coffee and slid an already baked apple pie into the oven to warm up. From the woodshed I brought in my two-gallon hand freezer with ice cream which I had made earlier, repacking it with ice and rock salt to keep the ice cream frozen soft enough to eat. The ice was from Mendenhall Glacier, only four miles from our farm. Before I left again for the barn, I poked two small pieces of wood into my wood-burning kitchen stove so that the pie would warm.

By the time I got back, Dr. Richard was applying a solution to Queen's leg to burn out the wound. "That prevents its recurrence," he explained. As he bandaged the leg expertly, he asked me to cut an old towel into four-inch strips. These he placed on top of his bandage, so as to hide the professional look. "When your men ask about the operation," he said with a smile, "tell them you did it."

As we walked back to the house together in the crisp autumn air, Dr. Richard commented on the beautiful moon and the sweet-smelling air.

In the kitchen we sat around the table with steaming cups of coffee and thick slices of apple pie, I felt the same relief that I saw on Joe's face. Our Queen would soon be well! "He looks so much more relaxed now," I thought. And I was glad for him.

Joe got his checkbook. "I can't tell you how much I appreciate this," he said. "How much do I owe you?"

Before answering, Dr. Richard spread soft ice cream over his piece of pie, and took a large bite. "I'd forgotten how good homemade vanilla ice cream is," he said. Then he looked up. "There's no charge. It was such a pretty ferry ride, with the moon reflecting on the water."

Joe started filling out the check. "I wouldn't give my milk away and you can't give away your services. You saved a valuable mare for me."

Dr. Richard smiled, shrugged and mentioned a very reasonable figure. As I poured more coffee into Joe's cup, I noticed that he had made out the check for quite a bit more.

The doctor began speaking about his wife in Ohio. "In her letter that came yesterday, she said she thinks she has a buyer for our house. After it's sold, she'll be coming to Douglas. I can hardly wait."

As the men got up from the table, ready to drive back to town, Dr. Richard said, looking at each of us in turn, "Remember, not a word about this evening. Much as I love horses, I can't risk getting the reputation of being a horse doctor."

No one ever found out what happened in our barn that night.

He and his wife lived in Douglas for many years, and he and Joe always exchanged a special smile whenever they met in Juneau.

April 25, 1933 — The Alaska Brewing & Malting Company has been incorporated here and is looking for a site for a brewery to fill the local beer demand.

July 14, 1934 — Yesterday afternoon the seven-place Fairchild seaplane recently purchased by Alaska Southern Airways arrived here to take its place in the company fleet. It was brought north by pilot Frank Knight.

July 16, 1934 — Two Army observation planes landed at the new Juneau emergency landing field near the Alaska Dairy yesterday at 4:30 P.M. These are the first planes to use the field since work started on it last week.

Chapter 12

Queen's Surprise

Finally our long-awaited summer brought us warm sunshine, so that the meadows and fields could dry after
our long rainy season. At last our hay harvest could begin.

"I'll start cutting tomorrow," Joe told me standing by the open
kitchen door. Glancing at the sky, he added, "There's no time to
lose now."

He sent one of his helpers to catch Queen and Nellie. Even
though we had two tractors for most of our work, Joe still needed
the horses to pull in the loads of hay. In order to gain time, he had
worked out a system so that there would always be one wagon in
the field loading while another wagon was in the hay barn
unloading. That meant two sets of crews. But we made better time
that way, in case the rain began again.

On that first afternoon, with all the commotion of getting
machines and hay wagons out of winter storage, my husband got
one of the biggest surprises of his life. Freddy, our milker, had just
brought the cows in from pasture. From my vegetable garden,
where I was weeding my carrot bed, I saw Freddy ride over to Joe
on Prince. He told Joe something. I couldn't make out what he said,
but it was obvious that Joe was uneasy.

His hat pushed back, Joe scratched his brown head a couple
of times. After a few minutes, he walked slowly toward me.

"What is it, Joe?" I asked, trying to hide my worry.

"Fred just told me Queen has a colt. Out in the pasture!
Imagine!"

"A colt!" Then I remembered that the previous autumn a
Morgan stallion had been in our neighborhood temporarily,
unloaded from a damaged ship. Mildred and Joe Jr. had brought

up the subject of breeding our Queen, and I, too, had eagerly supported their grand ideas.

But Joe had been adamant in his refusal. "Queen is not a young horse. She's never had a colt and I'm not about to take a chance on her life now." He told us to forget about having a colt on our farm.

Two weeks later the ship was repaired and the stallion was freighted to the Matanuska Valley.

"Well," Joe said disgustedly, "that darn horse must have jumped the fence without anyone seeing her and jumped back again — pregnant." He shook his head in disbelief at such a valuable horse like Queen giving birth to a colt without anyone there to help.

Very seldom did Joe see our horses close up after they went out to pasture, where they had plenty of nutritious grass and water. Oats they got only when they worked. From our house we saw them every day, prancing and frolicking. But even if Joe had seen Queen at a close up, he would have thought nothing of her swollen belly, because ever since we bought the tractors the horses had to work only during haying season. The rest of time they were on vacation, getting fatter and fatter every year.

"How is Queen going to behave out in the hay field, now that she has a young colt?" he said, thinking aloud. "She might even run away with the hay wagon to get home to her young one."

Ach du Lieber Gott! I said to myself. "Would she?"

But his worries were needless. Queen was as docile, faithful and obedient as ever. Only when it was time to unhitch her did she show eagerness to rush inside the barn. There her hungry colt met her, right at the entrance. My heart went out to Queen in gratitude.

At first I was careful not to let Joe see my delight in little Queeny. I hoped that after he got over his shock, he would begin to love the colt as much as the children and I did.

When Queen and Nellie were working in the hay fields, I would rush over to the horse stable and pat the sweet little filly, loving and talking to her. Then I would hurry back to the kitchen to baste roasts, prepare vegetables and salads. After I pushed a few pies into the oven (the harvest crew, too, ate with us), I would dash back again, trying to keep Queeny from being too lonely for her mother. She even listened for my steps. As soon as I opened the door, she

Joe Jr. and Mildred's playground. We adults sat in the gazebo, out of the sun, while the children played. Just out of the photo to the left was a swing set.

would gallop toward me in the greatest speed, so that a few times I feared that she would knock me down. But she never did. Always she pulled on her four little, stiff brakes in the nick of time. All she wanted was my arms around her neck.

Mildred and Joe Jr., too, were often in the barn petting and playing with the colt. She was a constant delight to us and so lovable

and beautiful. Her color was more that of a fawn than of her black-colored mother. Her little hoofs, tail and mane were perfectly shaped. Her legs were like straight sticks, protruding outward instead of being shaped like those of adult horses. When she nuzzled up to us, her small nose was as soft as a powder puff. She needed an enormous amount of love. The more we gave her, the more she wanted.

When Queeny was a year and a half, Joe started her getting ready to work. Every day, he would lay a halter on her neck, not fastened. Finally he fastened it lightly. To his surprise, she made no protest at all. Later came the collar and then the full harness. For a week he put collar and harness lightly over her head, taking it right off again. Finally she tolerated that, too. Joe, a very kind man, had immense patience with animals.

When he told me one day that he soon planned to hitch

Queeny and her mother to a wagon so that Queen could teach her daughter, I was very uneasy. I remembered his telling me that sometimes young horses refused, and tore up their harness and the wagons, even injured the driver.

So when Joe spoke of breaking in Queeny, I got scared.

"Suppose she starts to act up?" I questioned him. "Really, we don't need a third working horse. Nellie can continue to be Queen's partner. Why take the chance?"

"I've got that all figured out," he replied. "First of all, I don't want to feed three horses when I need only two for work. What I have in mind is to use Queen and her daughter to pull the hay loads and dispose of Nellie. She's not the most desirable horse to have around."

I realized I couldn't change his mind. But I couldn't get over my fear for Joe's safety when he would be standing on top of the wagon, trying to get young Queeny to pull it. How I worried about her training, wondering how it would go.

One nice morning Joe came into the kitchen, "This is the day I hitch them up. You can watch us. I'll take them right to the night pasture across the road."

I didn't know whether to hide or to watch. Getting more and more scared, I finally thought of going behind the house so that I wouldn't see anything. From there, to my surprise, I heard the smooth rolling of the wagon. Not at all jerky as I had expected. I came around the corner to look. I couldn't believe my eyes! There was Queeny in harness beside her mother pulling just as steadily as Queen! No resisting, no protest. I was so thankful! It was a miracle! A happy ending to what could have been a very sad event.

Gentle Queeny, who came to us by accident, brought immeasurable joy for many years to come. Truly a blessed event.

August 10, 1934 — Juneau's newest grocery, the United Food Company, will open its doors tomorrow morning in the corner of the Goldstein Building at Second and Seward. The company will carry a complete line of groceries, produce and meat.

August 17, 1934 — Ten seven-ton Martin bombers arrived at the Juneau airfield yesterday afternoon from Fairbanks and left this morning for Seattle. Except for the two Army observation planes that landed there a month ago, they are the first planes to use the field.

Chapter 13

Night Emergencies

In Alaska, daylight in summer is already bright at two in the morning, with sunrise at four. This caused our farm animals to be early risers. Having become a light sleeper after Mildred was born, I awakened easily to the animals' sounds. The sounds enveloped me with comfort and pleasure, soon lulling me back to sleep.

Great colonies of swallows flocked together at sunrise to perch on a 20-foot-long wire that was stretched from our house to a tree — our radio aerial. It was special delight to be awakened by a sweet song coming through our open windows. I loved to just lie there listening to their happy twitters and chirps until they finally sang me to sleep again. Even the huge runs of spawning, glistening salmon awakened me as they splashed in Jordan Creek that flowed past our house. I loved hearing their splashes and swishes as they busily moved rocks and gravel to build nests along the water's edge for their eggs.

Joe was a deep sleeper, and because he worked so hard and so many hours each day, I wanted him to sleep as long as possible. So, I tried to take care of problems whenever I could.

But when I answered a knock at 2:30 one morning, I had to call Joe. Through the window in the door, I recognized Charlie, a fisherman who lived 16 miles farther out the highway. He and his wife were both hard-working people. Together they fished in their gasoline-powered boat. Some of the fish they sold, and others they fed their slew of mink, housed in rows and rows of pens.

"I came to get your husband," he said apologetically. "Our only cow has been trying to calf for three days. But now she's so weak, she can't even get up."

An aerial view of our farm, about 1935. We were still living in the old house.

I knew they had a baby and an elderly, sick grandmother in their home who needed this milk.

"Tell Charlie I'll be right there," Joe said, as I explained the problem.

As the two men left the house, I heard Joe shout: "The milk house is on fire!"

For a split second I was paralyzed. Then I threw on my clothes and rushed out to help. Joe had called both milkers from the barn. They and Charlie carried pails of water to Joe, who was on top of the roof trying to douse the flames.

I shuddered when I got a whiff of the smoke. Flames were fluttering and crackling as they leaped up along the chimney.

"Hand up the pails," Joe yelled to me. He was now on top of the ladder. "That way I'll make better time."

The men ran back and forth with pails full of water from our large concrete, milk-cooling tank in the milk room. Luckily that room was not disturbed. Only the wood-burning boiler room was on fire. It was soaked from all the water that poured onto the flames, right down along the side of the tall, galvanized chimney, where the fire had started. A cinder had evidently fallen between the chimney and the dry, wooden shingles.

"I'll prevent that from happening again," Joe said. "This very afternoon I'll nail corrugated sheet iron on top of the shingles."

As Joe and Charlie were ready to leave, Joe saw me casting a fearful glance toward the roof. "No need to worry," he reassured me. "Everything is soaked. There's no chance for another fire."

Joe was already in the car, when he told the helpers, "You better bottle the milk today, and load the milk truck. I don't know how long it'll take me out there at Charlie's."

While I prepared breakfast, I heard Joe's car come into the yard. As soon as he opened the door, I asked, "How is she?"

"Fine," he said. "The cow is already chewing her cud. She got up shortly after I cut out her dead calf piecemeal."

"What happened?" I asked, seeing that his hand and wrist had red and blue marks on them.

"It took a while before I could get the calf out of her. I had to use the smallest blade of my pocketknife so not to damage any tissues," Joe explained.

Then he told me how the cow had fought his intruding arm. Her strong muscles, closing tightly around his wrist, felt like iron. "It sure is sore," he added.

I gave him a basin with hot water to soak in, and then I rubbed the wrist with liniment. Wearing an elastic wrist band gave him a little help. But he complained for a number of days.

I never ceased to feel amazed how Joe could accomplish such a feat and never harm the animal.

A year later Charlie and his wife Irma made a special trip to our house to tell us proudly, "Bess had another calf all by herself— and now is giving her full amount of milk!"

"Don't forget, Charlie," Joe said smiling, "thanks to your Bess, my milk house didn't burn to the ground."

January 5, 1935 — Joe Kendler, proprietor of the Alaska Dairy, has purchased a new International one-and-a-half-ton truck to be used in making his milk deliveries. His business has picked up to the extent that he requires a larger truck and bought the International from Service Motor Company.

May 31, 1935 — Juneau's new radio broadcast station, KINY, will go on the air for the first time this evening. Broadcast hours will be 8:00 A.M. to 2:00 P.M. and 4:00 P.M. until 10:00 P.M. daily.

Chapter 14

Mike Fox

F or the children and me the highlight of our day was Joe's coming home from his milk delivery route. Often we went out to meet him at the milk house, where he stopped the truck, to help him carry in mail, newspaper and groceries. Usually he was in a happy mood, just glad to come home.

But not on this day. The minute I saw him, I knew something was amiss. He looked downhearted.

"What's wrong, Joe?" I asked apprehensively.

"Old Mike Fox was arrested this morning."

"Mike arrested! What?" I tried to imagine 70-year-old, mild-mannered Mike in jail, with his pink face, hairless head — all pink, too — and those bright blue eyes.

"They had another drinking party in his cabin last night. He shot a fellow."

"Oh, no!" I exclaimed. "Did he kill the man?"

"Thank God, no." He went on to explain that the injured man was in the hospital. "But if that fellow should die," Joe said with a worried frown, "Mike will never see daylight again. Unfortunately, the shooting was not accidental."

Knowing how Joe felt about Mike made me feel sad, too. Mike had always been so ready to help us out whenever Joe was short-handed in the barn, even though he had no real need to earn money because he had both savings and a pension. He even helped us during our hay harvests in the summertime. Joe often remarked about the old man's industriousness and efficiency in spite of his having lost most of his index finger some years ago while working in the sawmill. He never stayed in our bunkhouse with the rest of our helpers, preferring to go home to his one-room log cabin alongside Lemon Creek, about seven miles north of Juneau. Mike always said he had to feed his dog, chickens, two pigs and two goats. Although Mike was a bachelor, his cabin was often crowded with people. He seemed to need companionship more than our other bachelor friends who lived in more isolated surroundings.

During winter months particularly, several unemployed sawmill workers or fishermen who had squandered their earnings during the summer were always eager to share a square meal with Mike. He always had plenty on hand to eat: salted fish, home-smoked salmon and hams, homemade sausages, garden-grown vegetables and game.

Since he made large batches of home brew, the parties were always lively. Evidently there had been one party too many.

Two days after Mike's arrest, I had a visit from a friend who was a matron in the women's section at the jail. Mary had made a special trip out to our place to tell me that she had heard Mike Fox yelling again and again, "I want to see Joe Kendler! Will someone take me out to see Joe Kendler?"

Mary told me, "Several times I heard the warden tell him, 'Pipe down, Mike! No one's going to take you anywhere.' But Mike kept right on yelling."

After Mary had gone back to town, I started preparing my dinner, still thinking about Mike, wondering what he thought Joe could do for him, or why he was so anxious to see Joe.

A short time later I glanced out the window and saw a police car driving into our yard. I hurried out, feeling uneasy.

Two policemen stepped out of the car. To my surprise I saw a third person get out — Mike.

"Missus, is Joe at home?" he asked hopefully.

"I'm sorry, Mike," I told him, wondering what he wanted with Joe. "He went to town to bring home a load of freight."

Mike was obviously disappointed, his deep blue eyes brilliant, his face ruddier than ever.

"Will you tell him that I want to see him as soon as possible?"

I nodded, feeling terribly sorry for him, with two policemen standing on each side, the outline of revolvers showing beneath their jackets. I felt I should not let him go back to jail without some friendly word of reassurance.

But I couldn't offer sympathy because the officers might think

This is Territorial Governor John W. Troy paying us a visit in the mid-1930s. From left, me, Joe and Joe Jr., Dave Hansel, John and Elizabeth Feusi and Mildred.

I condoned Mike's lawless conduct. So I asked, "Mike, why do you associate with people like that?"

"Why, Missus," the 70-year-old Mike answered almost indignantly, "That's because of *love!*"

When Joe came home I could hardly wait to tell him what I had learned. I told him everything, even before he got his coat off.

"So that's the reason for the shooting match," Joe said, nodding thoughtfully. "There's a woman involved." He paused, then said, "I'm going to see Mike. I'll be back in time for my chores."

In about an hour and a half he was back again. He told me that Mike had pleaded with him to bail him out.

Joe had written a $500 check, to be cashed only in case Mike didn't appear for trial. Joe was sure that Mike would be on hand.

Fortunately, the injured man got better, and Mike was free to go home to await trial.

Mike's trial was surely the shortest ever held in Juneau. Afterward, a friend of his drove out to our dairy to tell us what had happened.

The judge first reprimanded Mike. "Don't you know better than to shoot at people?" he asked.

'Your honor, it ain't easy for me to shoot anything. I can't use this finger." He held up his stubby index finger. "I had to shoot with my middle finger."

"Why shoot at all?" the judge inquired.

"Because of love," Mike said solemnly. "I kept telling that man to leave my woman alone. First thing I knew, he's running at me with my own ax."

"Case dismissed," the judge said.

September 28, 1936 — Excavation for the new Juneau Dairies building to be put up by the Warrack Construction Company at 12th and Glacier Avenue was started this morning. N. Lester Troast and Associates are the architects for the $30,000 building which will measure 45 by 95 feet. Juneau Dairies was formed three months ago by four local dairies: Juneau Dairy, owned by L. Smith; Alaska Dairy, owned by Joe Kendler; Mendenhall Dairy, owned by George Danner; and Glacier Dairy, owned by Frank Maier.

June 3, 1937 — Pasteurized milk makes its debut in Juneau the first of next week with Juneau Dairies, Inc., offering either raw or heat-treated milk to its customers. The plant handles milk from five local dairies: Juneau, Mendenhall, Glacier, Alaska and Peterson's.

Chapter 15

Horse Laugh

One of Joe's problems on our dairy farm was to get trained help. Because there was little or no farming in Juneau, there were few farm workers. The major industries were mining, fishing and government. None of these industries develop these skills useful in milking cows. So it was necessary to import experienced help from Washington State. Some of the men who applied, however, were opportunists, anything but farm help. Their ambition was to get to Alaska, come what may.

One time we were in desperate need of a good man. So when Charlie arrived, we hoped he was an experienced milker.

The first thing Joe asked was, "Can you ride a horse?"

"Sure," Charlie replied. "I'm quite a rider."

After lunch Joe and Charlie went out to the horse barn. I went out with them to collect eggs from a nearby hidden nest.

Joe led our brown Morgan out of the barn. "This is Prince," he said to Charlie.

"You don't need a whip," Joe told him. "He knows where the cattle are, and he gets there fast."

"Nice horse," Charlie said.

That was not exactly the word I would have used. Prince, though usually placid and good-tempered, still had a mind of his own.

Joe went on to tell Charlie about the time one young know-it-all wanted to show off his daredevil horsemanship, while riding bareback. "He kicked Prince's flank while mounting. Prince reared up on his hind legs, and the rider slid off."

I smiled, remembering how Prince had trotted riderless back

Joe and Joe Jr. sitting on the front porch of our new home. The house was painted a cream color with green shutters that was a nice contrast to the surrounding buildings in the lower photo.

to his stable, leaving the embarrassed milker on the ground behind him.

"Where's the saddle?" Charlie asked.

"In the horse barn. After you've saddled him it's time to bring in the cows," Joe informed him.

Charlie sounded a bit apprehensive, I thought. A minute later I glanced up from my egg collecting not far from the horse barn, and saw Charlie fastening the saddle cinch around Prince's belly.

Our new house and cow barn as seen from the back. That's Douglas Island across Gastineau Channel in the background.

Joe, a few feet away, was also watching. "Tighten the cinch more," he called out, "or you'll end up under his belly."

"Oh, yeah," Charlie said. "It's been a quite while since I saddled a horse."

I saw him tighten the cinch and then prepare to mount. Charlie's foot slipped from the stirrup. He tried again. By this time Prince, impatient at Charlie's delay, started to dance around. He snorted. He wanted to get going to his work, which he loved.

Finally Charlie was up. Prince quickly went into a gallop. Charlie's legs were stretched out, away from the horse, looking like a wishbone. Startled, I hurried over to Joe.

By now Charlie had thrown both arms around Prince's neck and was hanging on for dear life.

Disgusted, Joe threw up both of his arms and then pointed. "He doesn't even have his feet in the stirrups! If that's all he knows about horses, what in the world will he know about cows?"

Prince galloped only a few yards more before he had his fill of what was obviously a novice rider. Then suddenly, he stopped and dropped to his knees. Slowly, slowly he flattened himself to the ground — head and all — until he was lying on his side, his legs stretched out. Luckily, Charlie managed to get his legs out from under in time.

Our lone ranger, still mounted, looked around in bewilderment, "What's the matter with this horse?" he demanded of Joe.

Joe couldn't answer. He was laughing too hard at the sight of Prince playing dead.

"Come on," Charlie coaxed, shaking the reins. "Git up." Obviously he still thought he had a chance for our job.

Stubbornly, Prince continued to play dead.

With a resigned sigh, Charlie scrambled off. As he walked sheepishly back to Joe, he admitted, "Actually I lied to the employment agent about your job. I'm a cook by trade. I told him I was a milker because I wanted to come to Alaska.

Still smiling broadly in spite of our desperate need for a milker, Joe said, "Better stick with your pots and pans. I'm not about to let you practice on my cows. Up here in Alaska, dairy animals are too valuable for that."

Meanwhile, with Charlie off his back, Prince jumped to his feet. Even before Joe, he had known that Charlie wouldn't do. With a snort he galloped off to his stable. Just before he went inside, he turned, switched his tail and whinnied. I could have sworn it was a horse laugh.

August 20, 1938 — The first scheduled Pan American Airways air express flight arrived from Seattle today. The Sikorsky amphibian Alaska Clipper landed at Auke Bay.

March 9, 1939 — Telephone service from any home in Juneau to the wide world will be inaugurated tomorrow night. This will enable anyone having a phone to make long-distance calls without going to the radio office.

March 10, 1939 — The Baranof Hotel will have its formal opening this evening. The hotel has 96 rooms and 28 apartments and was constructed at a cost of $550,000.

Chapter 16

Duck Creek Field

"Monday morning we will have a go at it," Joe said to his helpers. "Clearing those 30 acres at Duck Creek will be a tough job; that timber is the heaviest around here."

I had known all along how much Joe wanted to clear that piece of land. He always stressed: "Only land that produces giant timber, like those huge trees, will make good farm land.

Three capable men offered their help to cut down the trees, and with a gasoline-powered engine, they sawed up the trees for firewood. Much of this wood was stored at our place, but a great deal of it was sold to people in the community.

When Joe and his men came to the house for meals, through their discussions of the work, I learned what an awesome job land clearing is. They spoke of steel cable breakage, tractor stalling and dynamite that failed to explode because of too much water in the ground. However, they never missed a day, rain or shine, except Sundays.

Most of the trees were tall Sitka spruce and hemlock. There were also some alder and cottonwood trees near the fringe area. Several Sitka spruce were 60 to 80 feet tall. Stumpage often measured five to six feet across. The men left a few of the tall ones standing to use as anchor trees to pull up stumps and roots with the aid of steel cables and a tractor. Joe said that the Sitka spruce posed the greatest pulling problem because of their huge diameters.

It required several years to dry and burn down the many stumps. Some of the really big ones couldn't be burned and had to be hauled away.

Now, another backbreaking job awaited the men — plowing the field. Countless roots that had been missed during clearing

We used this Frigidaire to keep the evening milk cool overnight. At the time, it was a real modern convenience.

Here I am feeding my flock of geese.

---

turned up constantly to hinder the plowing progress. Long and short roots, thick and thin ones became entangled in the double plowshares so that they had to be cut loose with axes. Finally, the exhausting toil ended, and plowing and seeding the field was accomplished.

Alaska's winter weather harms vegetation. Only grass with deep roots has a chance to escape damage, or, as in some cases, total destruction. For this reason Joe searched long and hard to locate winter-hardy species of grasses, which were Kentucky bluegrass, timothy grass, rye grass and alsike clover. All these varieties survived and thrived year after year.

About two years after seeding, the Duck Creek field produced profusely, just as Joe had predicted. We were more than pleased. Now, instead of shipping seven carloads of alfalfa from Ellensburg, Washington, every winter, at the cost of $7,000, we only had to order one carload for $1,000. The rest of the hay we harvested ourselves. Such a great accomplishment brought us much satisfaction and happiness. We now saw a way of getting ahead.

To give his field proper care, every spring Joe and his helpers applied heavy dressings of well-decomposed barnyard fertilizers. With spreading equipment they hauled tons and tons of it to enrich the land with humus and crop-growing nitrogen. After a spring rain had washed much of its value into the soil, Joe would use the tractor to pull the heavy, spring-toothed harrow and run over the field in all directions to loosen the soil around the roots to let in oxygen. The results proved to be great. Year after year we harvested tons and tons of wonderfully nutritious hay.

To see the fields full of ripening grass before harvesting was a real joy. Often the grass stood five feet tall and taller.

April 30, 1940 — In accordance with a vote taken on April 2, at midnight tonight Juneau residents will move their clock one hour ahead and thereafter the city will be on Pacific standard time.

November 10, 1940 — The Pan American Airways DC-3 wheel-equipped airliner, which is relieving the flying boat Alaska Clipper on the Alaska run, arrived here this afternoon from Seattle by way of Vancouver and Prince George. There were only CAA personnel and nonpaying passengers on this first trip over the route.

Chapter 17

Clean Clothes, Clean Money

Shortly before the United States entered the Second World War, help was very scarce in Alaska. Although we needed two milkers, we had only Fred; our second milker had been drafted, and we seemed to be unable to find a replacement for him.

Defense contractors were constantly urging men to work for them, as defense projects were being rushed feverishly toward completion. They offered fantastic wages, $1,000 a month for even unskilled workers, according to some reports. Fishermen, store clerks, farm workers, office workers, goldminers — all rushed north where the big money was.

It was during this critical time that Joe remembered Mike, an Austrian of about fifty, who had milked cows on the Alps. And since we used milking machines, the work wouldn't be so strenuous as hand milking.

Joe decided to go over to Douglas and talk to Mike. When he came back, he was filled with enthusiasm. "He's coming," he told me happily before I could even ask.

Two days later Mike moved into our bunkhouse. He was still a good-looking man, tall and slender with wavy hair that had started to gray at the temples.

At the dinner table he loved to entertain us with stories of his experience while serving in the Austrian army during the First World War when he had participated in the campaign against Russia.

Joe was pleased with Mike. He was industrious and gentle with the animals. Yet one day, after Mike had been with us almost a month, Joe came into the kitchen to tell me, "There's a problem developing out there." He shook his head, drawing his brows

A side view of our house with the summer lawn furniture; early 1940s.

together into a frown. "You know the Health Department won't tolerate soiled clothes in the boiler room. I've told Mike twice, but his unwashed overalls are still hanging there.

"In the barn," Joe said, still frowning, "Mike is clean. But instead of washing his overalls, he buys new ones. The dirty ones just pile up in the boiler room."

"Maybe you should ask him, again."

"I'd like to. But we can't risk losing him. He's never been married," Joe said with a smile, "so he's never been told what to do."

Later that day, while ironing clothes, I thought of a simple solution. I wasn't sure that Mike would appreciate it, but it was better than confronting him about those dirty overalls.

The next morning after the breakfast dishes were done, I decided to carry out my plan. Determined to wash all Mike's overalls, I went to the boiler room. With a piece of kindling I lifted those blue, filthy things off the wall hooks, one after the other, counting seven of them.

Grimacing, I reached reluctantly inside those clammy, dirty pockets to extract the accumulated nails, screwdrivers, screws, pliers, dollar bills, coins, cigarettes, matches, and a spool of black thread. I placed the salvaged objects in a wooden apricot box, then I filled the washing machine, which we kept there for the men's

Alaska Dairy
MILK BOTTLE

Out of the

COMES
HUSKY CHILDREN

▲

"Our Milk Stands Every Inspection"

Our dairy on the Glacier Highway is equipped with modern, sanitary milking machines and Frigidaire Cooling Systems.

▲

Cream Prices		Milk and Cream sold at
Gill	10c	SANITARY GROCERY
Half Pint	20c	GEORGE BROTHERS
Pint	40c	CASH GROCERY
		(*Willoughby Avenue*)

ALASKA DAIRY
Glacier Highway
JOS. KENDLER, *Prop.*

This was our advertisement in the 1935 Juneau-Douglas telephone directory.

Our dairy barn was an L-shaped building, with the building on the opposite side just as large as this one.

---

use, with lots of hot water and soap. After a moment's hesitation I added half a gallon of kerosene, preferring its smell to the other. With the same stick I picked up the clothes and dropped them into the suds. Then I placed the lid on the machine, with a fine feeling of satisfaction.

But as I stood there listening to the clothes swish back and forth, I began to worry about Mike's reaction. Would he be furious with me for interfering in his business?

All of a sudden he strolled into the boiler room, yawning from his morning nap. Somewhat jittery, but trying to sound cheerful, I said, "Mike, I'm doing you a big favor."

"Ain't that nice!" He glowed his pleasure.

"I'm washing your overalls." I put everything that was in your pockets in this box. Your dollar bill is right on top."

Mike stared at me, his dark eyes growing larger and larger. Just then Joe walked into the boiler room.

"Only one dollar bill?" Mike exclaimed. "Where's the rest of my money?"

I was startled by his violent reaction, his fists clenched, his accusing voice.

"There was no other money, Mike," I insisted uneasily, wondering why he would lie about it.

"Oh, yes, there was." He looked at Joe, who was looking at me for an explanation.

"I went through all your pockets very carefully. There wasn't anything else."

"There was $450 — in paper bills." Mike was yelling by now.

I began to tremble. Was he telling the truth? I was positive I'd gone through all his pockets.

Glancing at Joe pleadingly, I noticed that he was chewing on his cigar, a sure sign that he was upset. When he was happy or contented, he puffed away on it, showing his enjoyment.

I knew what was on his mind. We would have to pay Mike every dollar he claimed to have had in his pockets. What a terrible predicament I had got myself into!

"We can strain every bit of the wash water through a sieve. Even if the money is all in pieces (if there was any money, I thought), we can get it replaced."

Fighting tears, I dashed to the house. Back again with the sieve, I went right to the washing machine. The motor was still running when I lifted the lid. I took one look, and my hand flew to my mouth. Too startled to talk, I took one step backward, still staring unbelievingly into the machine.

The men hurried over to peer in. "Look at that!" Joe exclaimed. "The whole machine is full of money!" Both men began to laugh. I didn't know whether to laugh or cry with relief. I stopped the motor, picked out the money, rinsed off each bill under clear, running water, then I draped it around the edge of the machine to dry. There must have been at least twenty bills — tens, twenties and fifties. It was the most beautiful and cleanest money I had ever seen.

Mike was beaming. "Ain't that nice!"

I asked curiously, "Where did you keep the money?"

Patting his chest, he answered, "In my bib pocket."

"Oh, my," I said, "I never thought to look there. But don't expect me to wash your money every time I wash your overalls."

"Don't worry," Mike explained. "After this I do my own wash. I might even put my money in the bank."

April 2, 1941 — Feathers now flying over Alaska in the tails of bald eagles will soon be flying over Germany in the hats of the American Eagle Squadron of the Royal Air Force. A single eagle feather in the flying helmet has been adopted by the American fliers with the RAF as their insignia.

May 16, 1941 — Morrison and Knudsen Construction Company was low bidder on building the CAA airport near the Alaska Dairy, with a figure of $442,000. The job will require moving about two million cubic yards of material.

Chapter 18

Famous Visitors

When Mildred and Joe Jr. reached the movie-conscious age, they begged me to drive them to Juneau on Saturday afternoons, so they could go to the show before I drove them to their piano lessons. I would agree if they would help me clean the house. It was always my belief that children should assume some home duties and learn by doing.

I was pleased with their enthusiastic response. But even with their help, I was always in a hectic rush to finish before getting ready for town, since I also had to prepare a hearty lunch for the family and our hired help.

One forenoon, just before it was time to leave for the movies, the doorbell rang. Sure that it was a salesman, I rushed to the front door, ready to get rid of the unwelcome caller. Through the glass door I could see that there were three salesmen this time.

I was just getting ready to make my usual, "No, thank you" speech, when one of the men spoke first, "Mrs. Kendler?"

"Yes."

May I present Secretary Johnson and Captain Newmarker. My name is Johnson, too.

My perplexed mind turned a somersault. Secretary Johnson? Captain? Then I remembered the headlines in our local paper: *Twenty-five Top Officials and Congressmen from Washington, D.C., Arrive in Juneau to Survey Alaska for Defense.*

Oh, what a terrible faux pas I had almost committed. More than a little awed and confused, I managed to pull myself together, the matinee completely pushed out of my mind. Realizing that I was still peering at the men through a partially open door, I opened it wide, still wondering why they had come. Delighted that the house

Some of our dairy herd.

was in shining order, I stepped aside and asked, "Won't you please come in." Then I remembered that the tall, heavy man, with no hair on his head, but very strong looking, was one I had seen in pictures in newspapers and in various periodicals. He gave me an impression as though he could shoulder the gravest responsibilities— Secretary of Defense Louis A. Johnson. The other Johnson would be the Assistant Secretary of Commerce. "I wonder if we could get a couple gallons of coffee from you," he asked, holding up his strange-looking container, which I now realized was a very elegant Thermos. He went on to explain, "Our plane to Fairbanks ran into heavy fog and the captain had to return to the Juneau airport."

Overwhelmed, I managed, "Of course. It won't take me long to make your coffee."

I seated them in the living room and placed the latest Juneau and Anchorage newspapers before them on the coffee table. Then I headed for the kitchen. On my way out I heard one of the men say, "Oh! To take some of this invigorating glacier air back to Washington."

So that was why they didn't send someone for the coffee, I said to myself. They wanted to inhale our wonderful glacier air.

I was pleased that we were living in our new home, a really pretty nine-room colonial house built in 1936, the same year the airport was built. I felt pride in our expertly polished woodwork, in our mantle and French door of imported Philippine mahogany—that the entire environment was really conducive to perfectly restful relaxation.

As I pulled out my old, large, blue enamel coffeepot, which I always used for our picnics, from the lower cupboard, I heard the children running down the stairs and into the kitchen. "Who are those men in the living room?" their anxiety about the matinee obvious. After I explained, Joe Jr. said, "I'll run out to get Dad."

As I opened a new, two-pound can of coffee, I realized why I had received this great honor.

The governor and various department heads had wined and dined the visiting officials and accompanied them in a long procession of shining black cars to the airport. Naturally, after the plane took off, they had left. When the fog forced the plane back, the men aboard could not contact anyone in Juneau, because telephones and restaurants were still missing in our recently constructed airport.

Had there been a telephone, the coffee would surely have been brought from town. But since there was not, the three had headed for the nearest house — ours. Undoubtedly, judging from their remarks about our healthful glacier air, they had welcomed the short walk.

I decided I'd better ask how strong the men wanted their coffee, and it occurred to me they might like to see an Alaskan kitchen. So I went back to the living room. "I'm not at all accustomed to making coffee for Washingtonians. Would you like to supervise?"

Without a moment's hesitation, all three got up and followed me to the kitchen.

"Not knowing how strong you like your coffee, I would prefer that you add the grounds," I said, handing the coffee to the Assistant Secretary of Commerce. The way he went at it, I felt immediately that this was the way he preferred it. He was chatting and showing that he enjoyed himself. In fact he was the only affable one among them.

Joe came in, and I introduced him and the children. My husband, a very pleasant man, met the unexpected situation with his usual calm and easy manner, starting to chat at once with our guests. They asked about the dairy business in Alaska, about the

Joe and Joe Jr. using our new automatic hay loader, 1941.

weather, and cattle feed prices. The captain talked to the children about Washington, D.C., its many monuments and federal buildings.

My attention remained on the big coffeepot, which was taking a long time to boil. Suddenly I looked and saw Assistant Secretary Johnson standing at my refrigerator, his hand resting on the handle, his dark eyebrows raised. Looking a little meek and smiling sheepishly, he asked, "May I?"

Laughing, I said, "Please do." Fortunately my refrigerator, too, had had a thorough cleaning earlier that morning.

I wasn't really surprised at his request. It seemed logical to me that, as the second chief of the nation's commerce, he would be curious about what Alaskans ate.

I saw him staring at the sugared strawberries from our garden, the sliced halves glistening in their sweet juice. Then he took one step backward and explained, "Oh!" Turning to me he asked, "And what is this?" pointing to a pint bottle filled with our rich golden cream.

"It's cream, of course." I wondered why he asked. Maybe it was a hint.

"Would you like to sample our Alaskan strawberries?" I asked.

"Indeed I would!"

Joe quickly poured our rich thick cream into a flowered pottery pitcher. I filled three bowls with berries and carried them to the pleasant breakfast room that adjoined the kitchen. Then I invited them to the table. The berries looked even more deliciously red, drenched in their rich cream. To judge from their expressions, neither the berries nor the cream disappointed the men.

While they ate, I poured the steaming coffee into their two-gallon jug. Half an hour later they left, grateful for the coffee and for the berry treat.

Secretary Johnson complimented Joe on the layout of the farm, its neatness and our colorful, landscaped yard.

As they walked away, I suddenly remembered the matinee. I was about to mention it to Mildred and Joe Jr. But one look at their enthralled faces told me that our famous visitors had been far more interesting to them than the missed matinee.

January 17, 1942 — Major General Simon B. Buckner, chief of the Alaska Defense Command, has requested the Juneau City Council to pass an ordinance to prohibit the sale of intoxicating liquor to men in uniform or in the armed forces except between the hours of 6:00 P.M. and 10:00 P.M.

January 26, 1942 — Alaska's first air raid shelter has been constructed in the back yard of Dr. W.M. Whitehead from a plan developed by the British Air Ministry.

January 30, 1942 — The February tire allotment for Juneau consists of two passenger car tires, two passenger car tubes, five truck tires and nine truck tubes.

Chapter 19

The Army Comes To Juneau

For the love of Mike, what's that?" Joe exclaimed. "Take a look out the front window."

I looked. There, marching right into our yard was the United States Army! As the soldiers passed our house into our Jordan Creek night pasture, we could see they were carrying guns. Where had they come from?

It took us only a minute to go to another window where we could observe better. But by the time we got there, not one soldier was in sight. It was as if the earth had swallowed them. Joe had cleared that piece of land long before, so there weren't any trees behind which they could have hidden themselves. Naturally we were puzzled.

Later Joe learned that the Army had arrived during the night, set up camp on our land and dug foxholes all over our night pasture for their practice alert.

Not having any particulars, only wild rumors, we believed that the enemy must be here already, or was being expected. We felt uneasy. Joe went to town, purchased a money belt, withdrew money from our savings and from then on carried that belt right on his body. We were planning to take off. We knew that if the worst should come, our animals would be slaughtered to feed the Army. But meanwhile we might have a chance to escape alive.

The Army gave out no information. Only orders. Orders that civilians could not refer to soldiers or the Army when writing to relatives in the Lower 48 states. In front of our property, the Army had erected huge signs:

> *You are now entering a restricted area.*
> *Use of cameras and binoculars is not permitted.*

Joe among his Guernseys and Jerseys. This was when people were still wanting a deep cream line on top of their milk. Then, when the doctors said too much cream was not good for you, people wanted less, so Joe bought Holsteins, which produce more milk and less cream.

Guards were being stationed everywhere. Our own farm activities were being hindered constantly. One day Joe started up his tractor to harrow a 20-acre piece of hay land. Harrowing grass land, according to Joe, is always conducive to a heavier crop. As he drove, he saw a soldier standing in front of the gate. Joe got off his tractor, walked toward the gate to open it, and was confronted by the guard with the gun on his shoulder who said, "I can't let you go through here."

Joe replied, "All I want is to go in there to work my field. I am interested in nothing else."

The soldier repeated, "I have orders to keep everyone out."

Joe came back home with his equipment and said, "I'm wasting my time arguing with those guards. I'm going to post headquarters to find out what they have to say."

The colonel gave Joe several special permits, so that he could enter restricted areas to perform his work, unhindered by guards.

Meanwhile we became friends with about ten soldiers. Joe and I were delighted with this group of neat and mannerly fellows. We liked and trusted them so well that we invited them to come whenever they found time.

Joe paid them for work they did for him, and even though they did not want to accept pay, Joe insisted. And so they saved that money and some of their own pay toward a furlough home. It made us happy to hear them talk about home.

One day Jim Stewart from Louisiana said to me, "Would you be willing to write a letter to my mother? I know she is terribly worried about me, and I cannot tell her where I am. But you could tell her, as long as you don't mention the Army."

This is the letter I wrote:

Dear Mrs. Stewart,

Am writing this message to tell you that recently we met your Jim. He lives right next door to us and spends much of his spare time helping my husband with chores on our dairy farm. We both like him very much, and he says he likes my home cooking, too.

My husband and I send you our best greetings from Juneau, capital of Alaska.

Immediately a letter came in return, written by Jim's sister, a teacher:

Dear Mrs. Kendler,

You will never know what your letter did for my mother. She is a different woman. She always worried so much about my brother, but your letter stopped all that. We thank you with all our heart.

I wrote more letters just to let the boy's family know where he was and how he was getting along, and I accumulated a good-sized stack of grateful replies. What I found especially nice was when these boys offered to vacuum the house, or clean up the kitchen while I wrote these letters.

One day three soldier boys knocked on the back door. When I opened, they each pulled out $50 from their wallets and asked if I would keep the money for them. They explained, "We can never get to town in the daytime, and the bank is closed at night and weekends."

To establish a functioning banking record, I used a notebook with numbered pages, set aside one page for each man to enter his name, amount of money involved and date. Each man signed beneath my signature, and each man received a carbon copy. This was how I entered into a temporary banking arrangement during World War II.

The following spring our daughter Mildred returned home for her summer vacation from the University of Alaska in Fairbanks. Since we civilians had not been permitted to refer to the soldiers in our correspondence, she was completely unprepared to find our home surroundings occupied by the Army.

She no longer felt free to ride her horse, nor could she ride her bicycle, or even walk along the road to visit girl friends. Soon I sensed that a tension was building up. Something had to be done.

We began to plan parties. Mildred invited her girl friends from town and I invited our soldier friends. After dinner everyone helped clear the table, and soon singing and dancing was in full swing. Mildred played the piano so the others could sing. I was relieved when I noticed that the tension had left her, and she was once again a happy, young girl.

Among our soldier friends was John Kamp from Chicago, a handsome and likable young man who became a good friend of Joe Jr., who was then a junior in high school.

One weekend it developed that John spent his three-day pass with us, occupying our guest room, enjoying himself to the utmost, and also making himself useful to my husband.

When John and Joe Jr. returned from fishing that Sunday afternoon, they both approached me with a request that caused me to burst into uncontrollable laughter. Joe Jr. said to me, "Mom, John and I want to ask if you would go to post headquarters to ask the colonel for an extension to John's pass."

A more absurd idea was never spoken, I thought. But when I saw what my uninhibited laughter had done to those two young people, I very much regretted it. They both looked so crestfallen, so disappointed and so hurt, that I felt an immediate need to make amends.

"On second thought, I don't see why I shouldn't go to see the colonel," I said to them. In my mind I felt certain that I would get out of this without making such an outlandish request. But for the moment, however, it was necessary for these trusting young boys to save face, and it was up to me to help.

"When do you want me to go there?"

"Right away," John answered. "The sooner, the better."

"How about Wednesday?"

Both were satisfied with that day. I thought, this gives me three days to work on them and get me out of this foolish predicament. But I didn't get out of it. They kept me to my promise.

Joe Jr. said, "You don't have to worry, Mom. You know how to talk to those officers."

By Wednesday I was the unhappiest person alive. "Joe, what shall I say to the colonel?" I asked my husband wearily.

"Tell him that two of my best helpers were drafted and that I need help for the hay harvest. But in the future try to keep yourself out of jackpots with those kids," he said jokingly.

On Wednesday when I drove up to that huge gate at post headquarters, I felt an urge to turn right back and go home. But instead I parked nearby and walked to the gate. The guard asked my name and purpose for being there. As soon as he phoned in this report, a sergeant drove up in a command car to take me to the right place. From there on I learned what is meant by the term "going through channels," as I was guided from one officer to another. Finally I met the colonel, who was in charge of the post.

I expected to be told, "We are busy fighting a war. We cannot be bothered with women's fanciful quirks."

Instead, the colonel was polite and kind. When I gave him my husband's message, he replied, "I think we can do something for Joe. When does he want that help?"

By that time my nervousness was gone, and I opened my handbag to pull out John's name and serial number, saying, "This soldier understands our team of horses and he knows the fields. He could be most helpful to Joe."

Two days later John came over one evening, smiling from ear to ear. "Well, it looks pretty promising," he told us happily. "Tonight at chow three officers and my captain stood at the entrance of the mess hall talking together and all the while looking over at me."

The following day a sergeant drove John into our yard, and with his large duffel bag on his shoulder our friend John stepped out of the car, starting a one-month furlough at our place.

But I took Joe's words to heart and thereafter "kept out of jackpots with those kids."

March 1, 1944 — Flames swept through the main building of the Juneau Lumber Mills yesterday doing an estimated $200,000 damage to the building and the equipment.

Chapter 20

Fishy Fowl

Even harmless wild ducks seem to have robbed us of our peace of mind. When the Juneau Gun Club gave up their old location on Salmon Creek, they moved to Mendenall Valley, near us, along Gastineau Channel. We had no idea that their arrival would be the cause of such profound disturbance. As far as we were concerned, they had certainly selected the right place for their activities. We never saw any of the members, and we never heard their shooting.

But two or three weeks later, the game warden found a great number of dead wild ducks along the waterfront. These ducks had swallowed great volumes of lead pellets and had obviously died of poisoning. To avoid this tragedy in the future and to keep the ducks away from this area, game wardens installed an automatic gun that sounded off every minute — all day and all night. The method worked, but it raised havoc with our much-needed sleep. Annoying during the day, at night it was unbearable.

So, Joe went to see the game commissioner. The gun club moved farther out the road and quiet was restored to our lives.

The pride and joy of our barnyard fowl was a flock of white Emden geese and 25 white ducks. While they liked to nibble on grass, we also fed them heavily on grain and corn, hoping to supplement our meat supply for winter.

In the autumn when the feed was nearly used up, I would brine cut-up goose meat in a mild solution of rock salt, some sugar and a couple cloves of garlic. I baked the smoked meat in a moderate oven just before I served this delicious treat. My chicken and duck dinners I prepared in the conventional manner — stuffing the fowl with a tasty dressing and roasting them.

Joe and me in the living room of our house.

I'll never forget my first duck dinner, one I had so proudly prepared. That was before I learned of the nature of our ducks' behavior in Jordan Creek. I used to love watching our white ducks in the creek, having such a lively time swimming, floating and diving. Sometimes I saw them dive so deeply that their white tails stood perpendicular, looking like a flotilla of little sailboats. It used to be such fun watching them and seeing them grow up and thrive.

Early in the autumn, when their feed was running low, was the time to prepare them for the roasting oven and freezer. On the day I prepared this first duck dinner, I gave it my most loving attention, wanting to treat Joe and his helpers to a most wonderful feast. Satisfied that my dressing was the most delicious one I had ever made, I placed it in the oven.

At the dinner table, while the men were still buttering their corn on the cob, I cut off a bite, eager to taste it. Ugh! It tasted awful!

What a terrible embarrassment! Quickly I grabbed the platter, still full and rushed to the pantry with it.

"What's the matter with the duck?" asked Joe, looking puzzled.

"That duck tastes fishy," I answered, fighting tears as I sliced cold, leftover ham from the night before.

"Well, of course," Joe said. "They eat fish in the creek."

I soon found a way to eliminate the fishy taste. I kept the ducks inside a fenced-in pen with a washtub filled with minnow-free water for their daily swim. Then when I cooked them, they tasted like tame ducks should.

Finally our isolation ended in a welcome change. I was happy to see more and more people building homes near us. I soon formed many new and pleasant friendships, lasting to this very day in many instances.

Another happy consequence of new homes being built and new people arriving was that the wildlife moved deeper into the woods, and no longer bothered us or endangered our cattle.

Yet, there came a day when we were terribly upset because of a menacing domestic dog. He belonged to an Army captain who had brought this beautiful white Eskimo dog from Nome.

This vicious animal was a cattle chaser. He was constantly on our pastureland, running our cattle. No matter how far away we chased him, he still returned. He chased the animals so mercilessly that they frothed at the mouth and their milk production dropped by 10 gallons a day.

"My cows can neither eat nor rest," Joe complained to the captain, as he pleaded with the man to keep his dog off our premises. The captain promised to do so, but never made the slightest effort to carry out his promise. Two more times Joe went to post headquarters to talk to him, but it never brought any results. The cows dropped 10 more gallons a day, and we found ourselves in deep trouble. Obviously the captain didn't care what became of our business.

Then one morning Joe opened all the barn doors to let the balmy, sunshiny spring air into the building. Joe spotted the captain's dog entering the calf barn. Now Joe was desperate. He ran to the house, got his gun and shot the dog.

When Joe came back to the house and told me about it, I got jittery and worried. While Joe was telling me how the animal ran out of the barn, dropped into the ditch alongside the highway and died, I saw a command car loaded with officers speeding into our yard. They stopped near the milk house.

Ach, du lieber Gott. "What will they do to you now?" I whispered to Joe.

"Not a darn thing," Joe said. "Let them come in here, I have plenty to say, too."

I dashed into Joe's office to grab the milk book to show them the drastic reduction of our milk flow. The men were still in their car. Then suddenly we saw them turn around and speed out of our yard as fast as they had come.

Apparently his companions had convinced the captain that he didn't have a case against Joe.

April 8, 1944 — The Alaska-Juneau mine and mill will close down tonight at midnight putting between 225 and 250 men out of work. The mine has operated since 1897 and the mill since 1917.

Chapter 21

Where the Swallows Nest...

I n Germany there is a saying, *Wo die Scwalben nesten, dort bluht das Glueck.* (Where the swallows nestle, there, blossoms good luck.) But I remember once when the saying proved wrong, when the swallows didn't bring good luck.

One year spring came very early to Juneau. Even in Southeastern Alaska, frost in the ground seldom thaws completely before early May. But this year was different. Snow and frost were gone in early April.

On one of those especially gorgeous, sunshiny days, Joe walked into the kitchen with something special obviously on his mind. "I think I'm going to start plowing tomorrow," he said. "The weather couldn't be better."

Joe's enthusiasm was contagious. I dashed upstairs to open our bedroom windows to let in the glorious sunshine.

After my housework was done, I carried several flats of delicate flower and vegetable seedlings that were ready for transplanting out to my small greenhouse on the backside of the house. This work I loved as much as Joe loved his. I couldn't have been happier.

Suddenly I heard a flutter, a twitter and chirping. Looking up I saw a whole colony of swallows arriving from the south. Jubilant, I ran over to Joe. "Joe, the swallows are here! We'll have an early spring. For a change, we'll have a long summer. Won't that be great!"

"No, those are the martin swallows," he corrected me. "They'll be here only two or three days to feed and rest." Then he went on to explain that the martins migrated to the Interior of Alaska. "Only the barn swallows migrate to our region," Joe added.

Then I remembered the difference, the sweet little barn

Our house, with full landscaping. One of my greatest pleasures was gardening.

---

swallow with its split tail. Year after year they brought us so much joy.

About three o'clock on that lovely April day, heavy clouds started rolling in, obstructing our friendly sun. An hour later it began to snow, large, heavy flakes. In the absence of wind, the snow piled up fast. By evening there was almost two feet of snow on the ground. Disgusting!

After supper we were so tired that we decided to go to bed early. I went upstairs first and as I turned on the bedroom light, I screamed, "Joe, Joe! Come here quick!"

He came dashing upstairs, taking several steps at a time. "What's the matter?"

I couldn't answer, I was so shocked. The entire bedroom was swarming with martins — there must have been at least a hundred birds. Martins were perching everywhere: on the light fixtures, mirrors, curtain rods, door and window frames, pictures, bedstead and windowsills. I had forgotten to close the window when it had started to snow, and the poor birds had flown inside to find dry and warm lodging for the night.

"Turn off the light," Joe said, "or they'll hurt themselves flying around."

I clicked off the light at once and closed the door. "What will we do now?" I asked Joe.

"Not a thing. Leave the window open, and the birds will fly out at dawn," he said.

We slept in the guest room. When I awakened the next morning, Joe had already left for the milk house.

Not as confident as Joe about our unwanted feathered guests leaving by dawn, I opened our bedroom door cautiously. To my delight the room was empty. The martins had flown the coop. But my joy was short-lived. What a mess they had left during their nocturnal stay!

I never felt the same about martins again.

*July 27, 1945 — Sale of the Feldon Apartments
on Calhoun Avenue at Fourth Street to
Mr. and Mrs. Joe Kendler was announced today
by Mr. and Mrs. Sam Feldon.*

Chapter 22

Stories From Austria

"Joe, please tell me another Austrian story," I would ask during those long Alaskan winter evenings. Joe would enjoy an after-dinner cigar, and I would sit nearby, my hands busy with mending or sewing.

Joe's old home in Austria was in Salbach, a beautifully located alpine village, where life was simple and, in many ways, even primitive.

"What story would you like to hear?" he would ask.

"Oh, I like them all. But tell me the one about the gendarme." Joe would begin:

"Most of the time I worked on a dairy farm, which was high up on an alpine plateau, surrounded by a long chain of immense mountains and beautiful meadows. My job was caring for the cows and making Swiss cheese, which my employer exported."

At this point I would ask, "Did your Swiss cheese have holes? And how is that done?"

"Oh yes, my cheese had lots of holes," Joe would say. "Small ones and large ones. Every day the cheese is treated with a specially prepared brine. It is kept in an underground cellar to ripen. With proper mountain air and moisture, the holes gradually form." He also said that the alpine grass that the cows eat imparts a particularly delicious flavor to the genuine Swiss cheese.

He also spoke of how he loved to yodel, and how the echo would rebound from mountain to mountain until it gradually faded away. Then other men across the mountains, would also start yodeling, keeping the echo reverberating in the same manner.

"That was great fun," Joe said. "All of us keeping the alpine echo ringing."

I used to beg him to yodel for me, and he made a few attempts. But he said that he didn't like to do it without that echo. And Alaska's mountains, being so waterlogged, gave no echo.

Then Joe would continue, "Once in a while I worked for a sawmill owner, hauling logs, just for a change. The slopes were so steep that the teamster had to take great care to prevent accidents, especially when the road went down. The heavy weight of the load threatened to push right into the horses' hind legs. If that happened, then all would be lost. I had a friend who was killed with his team just that way."

"How did you manage?" I would ask.

"Well, I had to be alert every minute. Going downhill, my right foot had to turn the brake crank, while both my hands pulled the reins so tightly that the horses had to help hold back the heavy load."

"Did you ever have a close call?" I wanted to know.

"Not with my team or logs, but I almost drowned a gendarme once."

"Tell me about that."

"That was on one of those downhill pulls when I was so busy working, trying to save my team. Having to use both hands, I was unable to lift my hat to greet the gendarme who was coming from the opposite direction in a horse-drawn carriage. He motioned me to stop."

"He stepped out of his carriage, fastened his bayonet to the barrel of his gun. Then he reached up to where I was sitting on top of the logs to knock off my hat with his bayonet."

"What did you do?"

"I got so mad at that senseless fellow that I reached out with my right foot to shove him away. But the guy lost his balance, dropped his gun, and tumbled down the riverbank right into the water. Quickly I secured the reins of my team, placed blocks beneath each wheel of the logging wagon, and rushed for the gun, which I then placed on top of the logs."

I was terrified for him, even though he was sitting, safe and sound, in front of me. "Oh, my goodness, then what happened to you, Joe?"

"Not a thing," he said smilingly. "At that time in Austria the law was such that whenever a gendarme lost his gun, he became

We celebrated our 25th wedding anniversary at Salmon Creek Country Club,
August 19, 1947, with several friends: Judge and Mrs. Felix Gray,
Mr. and Mrs. Mark Jensen, Mr. and Mrs. Matt Halm, Mr. and Mrs. Henry Meirer,
Mrs. Mae Crowell and Mrs. Amanda Cook Galatti, Mildred and Joe Jr.

---

useless. He lost all his authority. No matter how it happened that
he lost his gun. His superiors asked him no questions. He would
simply be fired. And I knew that," Joe added.

"What did you do?" I wanted to know.

"I had to jump down to pull that gunless gendarme out of the
river, or he might have drowned. He couldn't get out by himself
because his shiny boots were too slick. But now I was king for a
few minutes."

"He said to me, 'Bitte mein herr (Please, sir), give me my gun.' "

But Joe told him, "Not until you make a promise never to stop
me again on a hill like this just so I could lift my hat to you. I need
both hands to hang on to my team."

The gendarme promised, and Joe was never bothered by him
again.

Another time Joe told me about the day when his Imperial
Highness Kaiser Franz Joseph and his Kaiserin Elisabeth came
through their valley. He said that all able-bodied people of the area
had been commanded to be on hand in their Sunday best to shout
greetings to their monarchs. "Loudly and repeatedly we had to yell,

'Langes leben dem Kaiser, Langes leben der Kaiserin' (Long live the Kaiser, Long live the Kaiserin)."

He added, "Of the entire shows I liked only the eight, white Lippizan horses that pulled their fancy coach. They trotted so beautifully. I also wondered how much longer that Imperial humbug would last."

There was one memorable incident on Joe's mind, though he was only nine when it happened. His father had left for America to earn enough money to send for his family, and also to send them enough for them to live on. But Joe's father got sick and had to enter the hospital and was unable to send anything for the family. When the tax collector came to collect property tax for their small farm, Joe's mother could not pay. The revenue man simply went into the barn and took their only cow. The mother wept and begged him not to take the animal because it was the only means for food for the children. The man paid no attention and left with the cow.

"There and then," said Joe to himself, "I'm going to beat up that mean man when I grow up." That intention remained in his mind for many years.

Years later, after Joe had gone to Alaska and established his dairy on Douglas Island, he went back home to Austria to visit.

Arriving in his village, he found the economic condition in chaos, World War I having ended about three years previously.

With American dollars in his wallet, Joe suddenly had become an Austrian multimillionaire. At the foreign exchange, for one dollar he received inflated notes of one million Austrian crowns! He said, "I just didn't have enough pockets in my suit for all that paper money."

To help out his two sisters, he filled their larder with several years' supply of food. For each he bought 200 pounds of flour, 200 pounds of sugar, 2 large hogs, ready to butcher and a good milk cow. The entire bill didn't even amount to 10 American dollars!

"No matter what I did or bought," Joe said, "my American money just didn't move. It was so depressing that I wanted to return to Alaska without delay."

Before he started his return trip, he decided to treat his relatives and the entire community to a big party. He told the innkeeper who was to arrange the affair, "I have to go to Salzburg for a few days. So I'll leave issuing invitations up to you. Please see that everyone in the community is invited, and that you have plenty of meats and other food, as well as liquor and kegs of draft beer on hand. I want everyone to be able to eat and drink as much as he wants.

"Though there were huge, luscious-looking veal and pork roasts, many of the guests ordered weiner schnitzel — an Austrian gourmet specialty — hot potato salad and hard rolls."

After the banquet, the dancing and singing lasted late into the night.

Suddenly in the far corner of the hall, Joe spotted the former tax collector.

"Joe, what did you do to him?" I asked.

"When I reached the round table where he sat," Joe replied, "I saw that he was old and bent. Suddenly, no longer feeling need for revenge, I asked him, 'Herr Bender, are you having a good time?'

"The old tax collector answered, 'Yes, Joe, thanks to your wonderful generosity, I surely am.'"

The cost of the entire party for 65 guests amounted to 7.5 million crowns: $7.50.

In Mittersill, near the home of Joe's sister, was a beautiful castle with 40 acres of land, 20 cows and some horses. The owner, Baron von Hochstatt, could no longer pay his property taxes on it and offered the castle to Joe for 20 million crowns — $20.

"For whom shall I buy it?" Joe asked. "For my relatives who couldn't pay the taxes either? I don't want to remain in Austria. So it would mean that I would have to send money from Alaska to pay taxes on a castle in Mittersill? Nothing doing."

A few days after the party, Joe left for Hamburg to board the SS *Hansa* for New York, eager to be getting back to Douglas.

April 29, 1946 — A site for the new Juneau Public Library has been purchased on Fourth Street opposite City Hall.

Chapter 23

Managing Alone

A farm wife has her own tasks. She seldom helps with the milking or barn chores. Her duties include the vegetable garden, food preservation, house cleaning, sewing and cooking for the hired help, as well as for the family. Yet, circumstances could force her to enter her farmer husband's domain.

It was nearly time for Joe and his men to come in to eat. So I was adding the finishing touches to my evening meal. I was just making the gravy when I heard the back door open — a cue for me to dish up the food.

Since the kitchen door into the hall was closed, I couldn't understand why the men were taking so long getting away from the entrance. I heard their voices, but couldn't distinguish what they said. It sounded as though they were carrying something heavy and were having difficulties moving it.

Curious to see what was going on, I opened the door. What a shocking sight! Tom and Reid, our two milkers, were trying to get Joe into the house. With one on each side of him, their hands beneath his armpits, they lifted him over the threshold.

"I hurt myself," Joe said. "I slipped on some ice and fell. I don't think I broke any bones, though. It must just be a bad sprain."

After we had him lying on the davenport, I drove to town to get the doctor, since there weren't yet any telephone lines out in the country.

An hour after I got home, I saw the doctor's car driving into our yard. Relieved to see him, I opened the door for the tall doctor, who then quickly diagnosed Joe's trouble.

"You've fractured your hip bone," said Dr. Dawes. "I recommend that you leave for Seattle at once. There's a famous bone specialist, Dr. Roger Andersen, at Swedish Hospital, who uses the new pin method to set broken bones."

He went on to say that doctors in Alaska didn't yet use this method. "But I highly recommend it for your case." He also said the SS *Alameda* was to leave the Juneau dock the following forenoon.

Even though I felt numb from the shock and fear, I at once rushed into necessary action. I had to go back to town to find a nurse to take care of Joe on the boat, make arrangements with the Alaska Steamship Company, buy tickets and hire an ambulance to take him to the boat.

The next morning I drove behind the ambulance. As the men carried the stretcher up the gangplank, Joe's nurse, Miss Winter, was already on deck to meet us in her white uniform. She had Joe's stateroom ready for him, his blanket rolled back. After the men with the stretcher had left the room, Miss Winter removed his robe, and brought him a second pillow for his comfort.

Although heavy-hearted, I felt relieved to have him in care of such an obviously competent nurse. I knew she would make Joe as comfortable as possible. Her stateroom was right next to his.

"I'll leave my door ajar," she said. "And since I'm a light sleeper, I'll be on hand right away when you need me."

There wasn't anything I wanted more than to be at Joe's side, but it wasn't possible. There was the dairy to look after, the dairy he had built up by such hard work.

"Please don't worry, Joe," I said after I kissed him good-by and wished him Godspeed. "I'll look after everything for you."

He smiled and patted my hand. "I know you will."

By the time I reached the door, I couldn't hold back my tears any longer. Miss Winter noticed and came running after me on deck. Reaching for my hand she said, "Don't feel too bad. In a few weeks your husband will come back as good as new."

I thanked her and left the boat to go back to my parked car. On the way home I wondered how I could ever live up to my promise to Joe — to look after the dairy. I had had no actual experience with cows. I was even frightened of them.

Of course, during table conversation among Joe and his helpers, I had picked up a certain amount of useful information. I did know that a great amount of good care was needed for these animals, who miraculously, it seemed to me, converted green grass, hay and grain into rich milk. But I had no idea where to begin.

In the past, the only time I would go to the barn was when I had something important to talk to Joe about. The cows, accustomed to men only and never having seen me very often, didn't like me. Of course, I saw to it that I never came there when the animals were out of their iron stanchions. But when they were secured, I would venture, now and then, down the middle of the floor, where I tried to make friends with them. Most of them pushed my hand away with their strong nose, except one big Holstein at the far end. Whenever she saw me, she never took her eyes off me until I walked toward her. Even before I got there she would stretch her neck way out so I could stroke it.

At home I changed my clothes and walked out to the barn where the men had begun their afternoon milking. I wanted to report to them how everything had gone with Joe. But as I neared the barn I heard loud voices inside. Tom and Reid were fighting and yelling at each other.

Fear-stricken, I backed away and went to the house. What if one or both left? What would happen then? How would I hire replacements? I wouldn't know if they were trained or skilled enough to handle dairy animals. Even Joe sometimes ran into trouble like that, although, of course, he always recognized the situation in time, before any damage was caused in the barn. But I'd never know the difference until the cows were ruined.

Leaning against the refrigerator with my eyes closed, I prayed, "Oh, dear God, please show me the right way."

After awhile I forced myself to go back to the barn. At the door I could hear them still arguing. But shivering in the brisk, cold January winter, I was determined to go in. At the entrance I coughed loudly enough so that they would hear me. They stopped yelling at once. I entered the warm barn and I greeted the men. Hiding my worries, I said "It's lonely over there in the house. Do you mind if I come over here and make myself useful?"

I told them I could feed and water the calves, and that I could sterilize the milk house equipment and the milking machines. All this had been Joe's work — morning and evening.

They both smiled. "That would be right helpful, Missus," Tom said.

I had another idea to keep them on the job. The first evening at the dinner table I informed them that we wanted to pay them an extra bonus of $100 — while Joe was away, with payment to be made as soon as he returned.

"Why, that's mighty generous," Tom said, looking pleased. Reid, too, showed enthusiasm. "We'll take care of the place just as if Joe were here."

I believed them. Joe often remarked on their efficiency. It looked as though we were making a good start.

Early one morning as I entered the barn to do my chores, Reid said, "Ma'am, Old Ma is lame."

Ach, du lieber Gott! Something else gone wrong. Old Ma was Joe's favorite — an eight-gallon-a-day producer. "A real moneymaker," he used to describe her to me. She had had five calves; three of which were already producers, some of them with their second calves to help increase this outstanding strain. Now she had gone lame and Joe wasn't there to care for her.

I knew something had to be done at once, but what could I do? Call a neighbor? I decided against that because it might offend the men. Since they had told me about it, that must mean that I should take care of it, just as they used to tell Joe when something was amiss. Only I didn't know what to do.

Unhappy about the situation, I walked slowly to the feed barn where Joe kept the medicine. Opening the medicine chest, I saw a bottle of disinfectant and remembered Joe once asking me to bring him a basin of warm water. "I have to treat a lame cow's foot." he had said.

I decided to do the same. I stood behind Old Ma, ready to treat her right front hoof. But then I became panicky when I got close to her huge, barrellike belly. Her neighbor's belly was just as big. Not only were they heavy with calves, but they had just been fed. What if they didn't want me there? What if they pushed their bellies together, as I walked past? They could crush me flat. Several times I tried to approach Old Ma, but always I backed away. After half an hour of this half-step forward and two steps back, I forced myself to hurry past the danger zone.

To my utter amazement the animals didn't move an inch. Still trembling, I tapped Old Ma's ankle lightly with my hand, and she obligingly raised it. Examining her hoof thoroughly, I found nothing

Here we are in our living room just after returning from a trip to Seattle.

---

foreign that could be causing the trouble. Then I placed it into the solution to soak. Meanwhile, not knowing where the trouble was, I gave her knee a good massage with liniment and then her shoulder, too, for good measure. Later in the evening I repeated the entire process. To my everlasting surprise and relief, the following morning Reid said, "Old Ma is O.K." To this day I don't know which part of her limb was lame.

One day, after Joe had been in the hospital about a month, a letter arrived from him with a very special message that brought first amusement and then relief. "This morning the head nurse came to my room and asked me, 'Mr. Kendler, what do you people in Alaska live on?'

"I told her we ate the same kind of food the people down here do. Then she said, 'The reason for my question, is that your blood count is always so perfect.'"

How relieved I was to read that! With such excellent blood, Joe's hip had a very good chance to heal perfectly. No longer did this heavy fear press on me quite so severely.

One Saturday night, after the men had gone to town to attend the firemen's ball, I heard a cow mooing. Since they were always quiet at night, I got up to find the reason — just as Joe had always done. I discovered a Guernsey in the maternity stall ready to calf.

I was panic-stricken. I remembered once I had gone out with Joe to help when a cow was calving. During the birth he had had to turn the calf, "because," he had explained, "the hind legs were showing first." That meant a hard birth. I also used to help occasionally by bringing a basin of warm water, soap and towels. Once I had to bring him a rope to pull out a calf during a difficult birth. I hoped this would be an easy one. I ran to the house to get a veterinary book and then ran back to the barn.

As the cow kept working and pushing hard, all at once I caught a glimpse of the calf's hoofs. Were they front or hind feet? How could I tell? I kept comparing pictures in the book with the ones before me. Then all of a sudden, *plop!* Right in front of my feet lay the newborn calf, completely covered in a plasticlike tissue, which disintegrated rather quickly. I pulled the little wet thing toward its mother, and she, with her long, rough tongue, cleaned her newborn from head to bottom, starting at the nose so it could breathe. After several unsteady efforts, the calf stood on its wobbly little legs and quickly discovered the right place for its first dinner. Happy with my success I went back to bed. Wouldn't Joe be proud of me when I wrote the next morning!

At last came the long-awaited letter from Joe, announcing that he was leaving the hospital. But, because the doctor wanted to see him once more before he left for Juneau, he was going to spend a few days with some Seattle friends of ours. He suggested that I send Joe Jr. down to help him on the boat trip home.

A week later a telegram from Joe announced that they would arrive in Juneau in three days.

I spent the next two days baking, concentrating on Joe's favorites, such as cinnamon and raisin rolls, chocolate pie and lots of cookies. For his first meal I planned his favorite — stuffed pork chops. Now and then I wondered how long he might have to use crutches. But the all-important thing was to have him home.

Standing on the dock late that afternoon, I watched the SS *Yukon* approach the wharf. While she was still too far away for me to distinguish among the passengers, I saw a man waving frantically from the lower deck. As the steamer approached, I saw it was Joe. How vigorous he looked! He must be his old self again. He wore a brand-new hat and a tweed overcoat, and in his hand he had only a cane. Standing there on deck alongside our son, who also was waving and smiling, my husband looked more like a well-to-do tourist than a convalescent. And there stood I, feeling completely exhausted from the many sleepless nights. What would he think of me?

He didn't even notice as he gave me an affectionate bear hug.

July 17, 1946 — The new Goldstein Building is now officially open. It was originally built in 1914 at a cost of $110,000. Gutted by fire on February 8, 1939, reconstruction costs were $350,000.

Chapter 24

A Christmas To Remember

Weeks before Christmas I always began my holiday baking — *lebkuchen, pfeffernusse, springerle,* fruit-cake and stollen. I also planned the special Christmas cheer for our dairy help. So that time of year I had to bake more than usual. How I loved the fragrance that welcomed me whenever I came back into the house from the outside. It always reminded me of Christmas in my grandmother's house back in Germany.

One Christmas was especially memorable. By then Mildred and Joe Jr. were married and living away from home.

It was the first Christmas in the 25 years of our marriage that Joe had been able to stay at home all day. Until then he had always gone out every day, including Sundays and holidays, with the milk truck. It was important to him, giving his customers his personal attention, even on Christmas. Often I resented it. But since Joe thought his going along with our milk driver was necessary for our business, I became resigned to that.

But finally the day came when Joe no longer needed to deliver milk. Three other dairymen in Juneau had joined him in forming Juneau Dairies, Incorporated. Right at the edge of town the four partners built a two-story concrete building with walk-in cool rooms for milk and freezers for ice cream. They had also installed modern milk-processing equipment.

Right from the start the new milk plant thrived. Because it used its own delivery crew, the four dairymen had more time to look after their own farms, which had remained in individual ownership.

I was particularly happy with this arrangement. The pleasure of having Joe at home all day long promised the best Christmas ever. I had gone all out with my Christmas enthusiasm. After Joe helped me decorate our tree, cut on our own land, he took two large, red paper bells and a spruce wreath I had made out to the bunkhouse to decorate the windows. I also had sent two dozen special butter cookies, each with a little hole to put a red string through. Joe hung these cookies on the men's little evergreen tree. They couldn't get over that. They had never seen it done before, they told me at lunch.

"Cookies hung on Christmas trees are one of my early childhood memories in Germany," I explained.

Since Joe and I had been invited to have Christmas dinner at the home of our daughter-in-law's parents, Madeline and Fred Bonnett, I prepared Christmas dinner on Christmas Eve so that we could enjoy it with our men. On the following day, when we would be gone, they could have delicious leftovers.

For Christmas morning I cooked a special breakfast for Joe and his men. The delightful aroma of pastry, mingled with the scent of the Christmas tree stirred my spirit.

Instead of the usual bacon and eggs, cooked cereal and toast or hot cakes, I served sourdough waffles, a plate of sliced stollen and a platter of oven-browned sausages and eggs. I was pleased to see how much they enjoyed my special treat. Joe patted me on the shoulder appreciatively. "That was a delicious breakfast," he said. Then he went to look after the water system. While washing the breakfast dishes, I watched the thick powdery snow swirl around so furiously by the wind that it looked like heavy fog. At times I couldn't see anything but snow. But I felt warm and protected inside the house.

As I stacked my dishes, I saw Joe hurrying to the house. I realized at once something was wrong.

"That damn bull Dugan has torn the ring from his nose!" he exclaimed with a frown. Since Joe swore so seldom, it was a sure sign of his worry.

"Go to the bunkhouse and tell the men to stay away. I've got to be alone with Dugan. If he goes on a rampage, he'll hurt somebody," Joe said.

Why did such a terrible thing have to happen on Christmas Day! I was frightened by the thought of Joe alone in the barn with the bull. "What are you going to do, shoot him?"

"I can't shoot an expensive purebred Holstein like that," Joe

*Joe haying with Joe Jr. and Betty and their daughter, Debbie, 3, riding on top.
That's Ron Hurlock, one of my 4-H boys, with the pitchfork.*

said firmly. "We'll have to keep Dugan another year or so, our small bull is still too young. No, I'll think of some way to get the ring back in his nose." Then he rushed out.

Ach du lieber Gott! What a Christmas Day this was going to be, I thought as I put on my overshoes, a woolen stocking cap and a heavy coat. I hurried out to the bunkhouse through swirling snow. With a shiver I remembered how that mean bull hated me. Whenever I had to go to the barn that bull snorted, bellowed and pawed, as if to snuff out my life that very moment.

At the bunkhouse the men were surprised to hear my message.

"He's one of the meanest bulls I've ever seen," said Mike. "But Joe is right. We don't dare get near that animal without his ring."

"Dugan goes wild whenever anyone except Joe comes into the barn," Reid added. "But when Joe comes near him, he lowers his head to get it stratched. But he won't let any of us near enough to touch him."

I knew there was nothing I could do to help, but I still had to be at the barn. I pressed my ear against the door. Now and then I could hear the 2,000-pound beast lumber past, with Joe close behind, coaxing, apparently trying to keep the bull occupied. "Go on, Dugan. Go into your stall. Hurry up, keep going."

It was obvious he wasn't succeeding. Evidently Dugan was enjoying his freedom. Without the ring in his nose, he was master.

I really can't say how long they went back and forth like that. Joe coaxing all the time. It seemed like hours. Chilled from the steady wind and snow, I had to go back to the house now and then to change to drier clothes and to thaw out. Once I wrote a note to our milkers: "Lunch is in the oven. Please help yourselves." Then back to my listening post I went.

The wind kept on howling, whirling loose snow around and over me, even forcing me against the barn door.

At last all was quiet. Frightened, I pictured Joe lying inside, injured or dead.

Suddenly the barn door opened. Out stepped Joe.

"I got him in!" he explained triumphantly.

I was so relieved to see him that I was crying and laughing at the same time. Bent over against the buffeting wind, we walked to the house together, arm in arm. "How did you do it," I asked.

"Well, I had the idea in mind all along," Joe said, tightening his arm on mine. "But Dugan wasn't hungry enough. Finally, I filled his pail, he rushed into his stancheon. I slammed it closed."

"But the ring? How did you get it back into his nose?"

"I hid a sharp-pointed hay hook beneath his grain and held out the pail," Joe explained. "As soon as he pushed his nose into the pail, I forced the hook up his nose to make another hole. As I slowly pushed back the hook, I replaced the ring."

I listened to the incredible story, imagining the bull's pain, its bellow, how it must have flung its head. "It was a chance in a hundred, even a thousand!"

Joe nodded and said, "I had to take that chance."

I looked at the clock. "There's just enough time to get dressed for dinner."

It had been a memorable Christmas. What a story we would have to tell when we arrived at the dinner party!

September 3, 1953 — The Mendenhall 4-H Club for boys will hold their monthly meeting Saturday, September 5, at 8 p.m. at their club house on the Kendler ranch. The coming 4-H Fair and preparing exhibits will be the main topics. (Daily Alaska Empire)

October 28, 1953 — Gastineau Channel had its first snow of the season during night, but it was mixed with a little rain. Skiers are delighted as they look at the white hills around Juneau, and young sledders are hopeful for a greater covering of the white stuff on their sliding hills.
(Daily Alaska Empire)

April 3, 1953 — Hundreds of Gastineau Channel people called at the Governor's House last night to meet and congratulate governor-designate B. Frank Heintzleman at the reception given by Governor and Mrs. Ernest Gruening.
(Daily Alaska Empire)

Chapter 25

We Retire

One morning, after getting up early to do the milking, Joe rushed in from the barn, ready for breakfast. "I'll just wash up and be right back," he said. "I've something important to tell you."

As I made coffee and fried bacon I wondered what had happened out in the barn. A visitor? Did it have something to do with milkers?

Joe's oatmeal was steaming in the bowl by the time he returned. As he sat down and poured thick cream over his oatmeal, he motioned me to sit down, too.

"Now tell me what's so important," I demanded as I poured coffee for him.

"Well, I had lots of time to think while I was moving the milking machines from one cow to another — about what that new liquor store has brought us — nothing but trouble for four months. Before it came, the milkers seldom got drunk." Joe reminded me that it was the third time in a month that our help had gone on a drinking spree.

"So I have decided we should retire from the dairy business," Joe said. "We shouldn't have to struggle like this anymore."

"Retire!" I blurted out. "Do you mean to sell out?"

"No, no, not sell out. Just get rid of the animals."

Joe was so keyed up that he talked on and on. I was shocked, remembering how much he loved his cows, how proudly he kept everything in smooth-running order, how each year he had filled our large hay barn with our own cured, luxuriant and nutritious hay — tons and tons of it, up to the high rafters — and so removing heavy pressure off our finances.

In 1952 I won the Homemaker's prize for my home-canned spinach, salmon, halibut, beef and sauerkraut. That was also the year I was the chairwoman for the women's section of the Alaska Farm Forum.

Joe and me, 1958.

Joe had cleared 30 acres of our fertile timber land of thick underbrush and huge trees and then had experimented to get just the right mixture of grass seeds. It had been such a great relief not having to import that expensive hay from eastern Washington.

Without his dairy herd, I wondered how Joe would keep busy?

"Well," he finally said, looking intently at me. "Don't you have anything to say to the news? You know we won't have to worry about money."

"I'm not worrying about money," I told him slowly. "I'm worrying about you. You've been so busy all these years, how can you be happy if you aren't busy?"

He thought for a while and then said, "Oh, I'll find something to keep me going, all right," he assured me.

And so it was decided that we would dispose of our cows and young stock. That alone would keep Joe busy for some time. Meanwhile, I kept hoping we could find something for him to do so that he wouldn't have too much idle time on his hands.

One day at dinner I suggested, "Maybe we could fill the barn with chickens. To make the work easy, we could install automatic

Joe sacking potatoes. Joe's idea to grow potatoes commercially after we retired from the dairy business was a good one.

equipment of feeders and waterers, even an automatic timer to turn the lights on early. That way they could get up to feed and start laying while we're still asleep. How about it?"

"Not a bad idea," Joe remarked, nodding approvingly. "That way we'd be using the building. Maybe we'll try it after I sell the rest of the cows."

One beautiful autumn day, after Joe had disposed of his last cow, he rushed into the house to spring another surprise. He always liked to discuss important matters with me.

"What would you say," he asked excitedly, "if I plow under 10 acres of hay land and let it lie fallow over winter?"

"What for?" I wondered aloud.

"Well, I'd like to plant it in potatoes."

I threw up both hands. *Ach du lieber Himmel!* "Ten acres of potatoes! We'll have to have help again!"

"Of course," Joe said, "but only for a few days during harvest, the rest of the time I can handle it myself and still keep banker's hours." He smiled at the prospect.

Although glad that Joe had discovered something to keep his

Mathilde shows her potatoes to Clyde Sherman, seated, Clarence Holman and Dr. Allan Mick at the Alaska Farm Forum in Palmer. Courtesy of the author

mind and body busy, I wondered whether he should, at the beginning, go into it on such a large scale.

I remembered when an early frost had almost ruined our household potato crop. Such an unusual cold spell could happen again. But I didn't want to discourage Joe. So I wrote to the Alaska Department of Agriculture to ask for help in growing potatoes commercially.

At least we had our apartment building, a two-story building,

For more than 10 years I was leader of the Mendenhall 4-H Club. Three years in a row our float won top prize for originality in the Fourth of July parade. The $600 prize money bought a stereo and records that all 4-Hers in the community could use.

so ideally located between the State Office Building and the new Federal Building that it never lacked desirable tenants. In case of crop failure, I thought, the rent money would see us through without having to dig into our savings we had put aside for our old age.

One day, after returning from town, Joe came into our kitchen holding a fistful of mail. "Here's everything we need to know about growing commercial potatoes."

He sat down at once to study the material. I dropped everything, eager to get involved. For once I could fully participate in our new farming program, learning alongside Joe. I never had learned our dairy business. It was not only too complex, 1 had had my hands full with four hungry working men to worry about, my husband and children to feed, taking care of our vegetable garden and canning. But now, our son and daughter were married, and there were no more barn helpers to feed. I, too, needed something to keep me busy.

All through the winter we studied the pamphlets, again and

Traveling 4-H Delegation from Alaska Impresses Newspaper Reporter in States

By LOUIS R. HUBER

SEATTLE—Three sure-enough pioneers from America's last frontier—Alaska—went through this city recently on their way to Chicago to attend the National 4-H Club Congress.

In their baggage, a parka . . . and a problem.

"The parka is picturesque—it gets us plenty of attention," explained Mrs. Carol Winey, home-demonstration agent from Anchorage, who accompanied the 4-H trippers.

"The problem," she said, "is to keep people from thinking the parka is typical."

The real achievement of youth in Alaska is not in wearing parkas—which are about as numerous as mink coats in the States —but in doing the same sort of things 4-H members do in the States, added Mrs. Joe Kendler, 4-H leader from Juneau, who also accompanied the youngsters.

Mrs. Kendler, who arrived from Germany 33 years ago, can speak with authority; for, with her husband, she took up the pioneer challenge up north at about the point where the sourdough of '98 left off.

The Kendlers established a very successful dairy at Juneau, in an area where nearly all foodstuffs were shipped in to meet the demand of a gold-mining economy.

Recently the Kendlers "retired" from the arduous dairy work—to make just as large a success of raising potatoes and poultry . . . again, doing something that had never been done before in that part of Alaska.

When the 4-H ("head, heart, hands and health") movement was started in Juneau a few years ago, Mrs. Kendler became its mainspring.

The fact that two of the Alaska delegates to the Chicago gathering this year come from Juneau speaks for the effectiveness of her efforts.

Don Hurlock, 18, and Henry Jenkins, 17, the two Juneau 4-H delegates, have been so successful in their 4-H work that they might almost be termed businessmen.

Don's 4-H poultry project has netted him $3,700 over a three-year period. Henry won his trip with a garden project that included 15 varieties of vegetables—in an Alaska area, remember, where nobody ever bothered with vegetables before.

Equally impressive is the 4-H work of Lura Peck, 15, who comes from much farther north—Seward —and who won her trip to Chicago by outstanding clothing achievement.

In the five years she has been a 4-H member, Lura completed 173 sewing, baking and handicraft products. She now makes nearly all her own clothes.

These are not the first 4-H members in Alaska to win trips to the annual nation-wide 4-H gathering. Since 1947 Alaska youngsters have been delegates —but that particular date carries a special significance.

It is approximately the time, most students of Alaska agree, when Alaska residents who intended to make the northland their permanent home began to outnumber those who regarded Alaska as a place of temporary sojourn while earning a living.

The 4-H members have had more than a little to do with this change. They have proven that social roots can be well nurtured in Alaska soil.

Don Hurlock, for example, undoubtedly would become a successful poultry farmer anywhere—but he knows it is actually more profitable in Juneau.

"We have to rely on shipped-in feed at higher prices," he told this reporter, "but we get 70 cents a pound for fryers and a dollar a dozen for eggs."

The first 4-H club in Alaska was organized at Fairbanks in 1930; today there are 50 clubs, with approximately 500 members.

The "farm belt" running from Seward through Homer, Anchorage, and Palmer to Fairbanks has the most activity—but Juneau now has six clubs, and this year for the first time won national recognition for Southeastern Alaska.

"Our greatest anxiety in coming to the States is to avoid giving the impression that 4-H activity up in Alaska is different from 4-H work anywhere else," said Mrs. Winey, whose home town is Elgin, Ill., and who is a graduate of Iowa State College.

"The really unique aspect of 4-H work up north is that there is so much of it," she said.

A very important feature of Alaska 4-H work is its potency in combatting juvenile delinquency—an affliction that is unfortunately more serious there than in the States.

"We have never heard of a 4-H Club member getting into trouble with the police," observed Jessen's Weekly, of Fairbanks, in an editorial dealing with juvenile delinquency.

Racial tolerance also is encouraged by the 4-H movement up north. In Fairbanks all races are represented in several 4-H clubs. At Minto, near Fairbanks, a 4-H girls' sewing club is made up entirely of Athapascan Indians—as is the entire village.

At Juneau a boys' 4-H Club sent 50 pounds of seed potatoes to the Hydaburg Garden Club, more than 200 miles to the south, where the population is almost entirely of Haida Indians.

The trips to Chicago are made possible for Alaska 4-H winners by funds donated by various individuals and commercial firms, located mainly in the States.

Reprinted with permission from The Independent, *December 9, 1954.*

again. For years we had grown potatoes for our own use, but although delicious and good keepers, they lacked smooth skin and were badly spotted. They would not have been acceptable for commercial use.

One day Joe looked up from one of the government pamphlets and exclaimed, "Now I know what was wrong with our potatoes. For a smooth skin, the ground must be slightly acid."

"So that's why ours were always so rough." I came to read over his shoulder.

Joe pointed at another paragraph. "To supply the soil with needed humus, we'll have to plant oats and vetch. After they're a foot and half tall, they're plowed under. Then the field lies fallow for a year."

"So we need two fields, if we harvest every year," I said. "One to plant and one to lie fallow."

We did plant potatoes and were successful, too. Just as with the dairy business, Joe worked hard and kept things running smoothly. But things were changing in Juneau and we were getting older. We decided to move to Washington.

"Joe, do you think we could ever love another place as we did our farm?" I asked my husband sadly. Sadly, because we were already packed. We were waiting for the moving men to take our belongings to a freighter. The next day we were to fly to Seattle to search for a new location for our future home.

"Washington is a very nice state," Joe told me. "Remember I used to work there, before I came to Alaska. It'll be easy to be happy there." Joe's brown eyes reflected his own sadness at leaving, but also an optimism that cheered me.

"That supermarket developer offered us a good price. So, the only sensible thing to do was to sell," he added.

"But I'm afraid," I admitted. "After years of living here on this farm. Now, suddenly, we must break away, leave our many wonderful friends behind — go live among strangers."

"Well, you'll see, we'll make new friends," Joe consoled me. "And we have to think of our future."

"I guess so," I said. "But I wonder where we'll land."

As I looked out the window, I saw the moving truck drive up. Joe headed for the door. Just before he went out he said with a smile, "We'll be happy no matter where we'll go."

Glacier Family Couple Demonstrates How Deep Roots May Be Put Down in Developing Alaska

By ALICE B. SCHNEE

In Alaska today there is such a rush to surge forward into the 'nown and unknown and to sometimes think of the "last frontier." Alaska, as somehow sprung full-lown on the date of statehood. 'an. 3, 1959, that it is well to pause and remember and pay tribute to the hardy folks who pioneered or in any way assisted in the early 'evelopment of the Territory and State of Alaska.

Joseph and Mathilda Kendler are wo of these people who have lived a rich full life in Glacier Valley Mile 9, Glacier Highway, near the Juneau Municipal Airport. Here they have lived since 1923, thirty-eight years, raising their family, developing the dairy farm, taking great part in community endeavors, and finally selling most of the land for projects to develop the area, but remaining in their spacious colonial home which was built in 1936. These two people have now retired, just re-oriented their live to less strenuous activities.

To Alaska

Mathilda left Germany in the summer of 1921 to live with an aunt in Chicago, making passage on the Hamburg liner, SS Hansa, and there on steamer she met Joseph Kendler, who had been visiting his old home, Weinheim near the Rhine River. Joe was returning to Douglas, where he had employment on a dairy farm above the Gastineau School. In August 1922, Joseph and Mathilda Kendler were married in the John Feusi home, Douglas, with Mamie Feusi (Jensen) as bridesmaid.

Dairy Farm

In 1923 the Kendlers moved to Glacier Valley near Jordan Creek purchasing the 320-acre farm from Tom Knudson, the original home steader. Later they bought 40 additional acres from the government with soldier's script, and making their land extend up to the Charlie Cudy property on the Loop Road. The Knudson son, Herb, now chief mechanic at the Northern Commercial Co., stayed with them for 1½ years as their main help.

On the dairy farm, the Kendlers built up a herd of Holstein cows for production and Guernseys for richness, which they kept until 1952. In 1936 Joe Kendler was one of the original organizers of the Juneau Dairies, Inc. At the peak of their dairy operations, they employed four men, two as milkers, one as delivery man, and one as farm hand. Shortly after they started the farm in 1926 they bought the first milking machines; in 19 1 they added a Frigidaire milk cooling system, the first to be installed in Alaska.

The farm buildings included a dairy barn with concrete up to the windows, horse barn. calf barn and hay barn, milk house, bunk house, and the main house.

Country Neighbors

In the early days, only five families lived in that general country vicinity: the Vic Spauldings at Auke Bay; Albert Petersons at mile 11, the Charles Rudys on the Loop Road; the Kendlers; and the Martin Lynch's. These people petitioned for a school bus and it was granted to carry the eight children to Juneau.

The two Kendler children were born in Glacier Valley: Mildred. '2-23-23, and Joseph Jr., 4-24-25. Mildred is Mrs. Dale Steen of Seattle and has three children, Trudy, '5, Ted, 13, and Heidi 4. Joe, Jr. lives in Juneau with his family, wife, Betty Bonnett Kendler, daughter of the Douglas family, the Fred Bonnetts, and their two daughters, Deborah Ann, 11, and Sandy, 6. Joe Jr. is employed as a pilot with the Alaska Coastal Air lines.

Wagon Road

The Glacier Highway, was at that time merely a wagon road, without the benefit of paving or snow plowing: the road was not developed until the years of World War II. when the Army camp at Duck Creek made it imperative that the road be widened and surfaced. Frequently, in taking the milk for home deliveries in the winter, when the snow was heavy. Joe Kendler had to use the team of Belgian horses hitched to a bobsled, in place of the truck.

Farm Canning and Preserving

In addition to the dairy farm work, the Kendlers grew a sizeable 'arden, producing fruits and vegetables for canning potatoes and other root vegetables for the root cellar; also they raised chickens canned and smoked beef, ducks beef and pork, and made their own sausage. This preserving of food was an important aspect of farm life in the early days, not only for economy in using what 'oods were available, but because 'resh fruits and vegetables were not plentiful via steamship from Seattle. No cold storage or coolers were in Juneau at that time.

Mathilda Kendler, except for 'rowing of potatoes and hay which was Joe's province, was the gardener of the family. Under her direction and care the vegetables 'lourished, and she even developed a small but effective orchard attached to the house. They secured fruit trees—apples and cherries - from No. Dakota, and they thrived. Other trees ard bushes included 4 English Hawthorn. Mountain Ash. Siberian Pea Trees. Honey-

suckle, Climbing roses, and perennials.

In years gone by, Mrs. Kendler made and sold ice cream to the Alaskan Hotel and to George Brothers Grocery, making three kinds of ice cream, vanila. chocolate and strawberry; and sherbet, lemon orange, and pineapple. The Martha Society of the Northern Light Presbyterian Church had ice cream socials at the Kendler farm, and the Juneau Woman's Club enjoyed social affairs and meetings out there, with ice cream served as a special treat.

Children's Fun

The children in the country in Glacier Valley had lots of fun playing on Jordan River, boating and fishing in summer, and ice skating in winter. And, in addition the Kendler children had fun enjoying and sharing their two Shetland ponies, "Peanuts," w h o m Mildren trained to lift her hoof to shakehands, and "Teddy." Grit, Rod and Betty Nordling were three of the Juneau young people who had many good times in riding the ponies. The yard also held much play equipment, filled almost every day in the summer by chil dred from Juneau.

Later Years and Today

In 1936 the Kendlers built their present spacious colonial home and in the past twenty-five years have shared it with their family and many friends. The old home became a bunk house for the hired men and later. a club house for the Mendenhall 4-H Boys. The Kendlers over the years sold much of their property, first to the Army for part of the Duck Creek Camp; then to various interests for subdivisions, such as Airport Acres and Cascade Manor; and the land on which the Juneau Municipal Air port is located. The most recent sale, of 12 acres, was to a local group for development purposes. leaving the Kendlers their house. and about 2¼ acres surrounding it. The farm buildings are being tron down to make way for progress, as the great boom in housing in the country area demands more service stores.

Semi- Retirement

Neither Joe or Mathilda Kendler are really retired, though they no 'onger have the heavy burdens of a farm. Joe, at 75, is content to enjoy his good health, his cigars, and T. V., his many friends and man's chores about the house and yard.

Math: a is thoroughly excited about her new career in teaching sewing at the Community College. Juneau, which she began three years ago. Wednesday, she start teaching another series of 19 lessons in the Bishop Method of sewing. two times a week in the evenings. She teaches Basic. Intermediate. Tailoring and Fitting and classes. This interest started as an outgrowth of her activities in the Mendenhalt Home-maker Club and associations with the University of Alaska extension short courses. They lead to participation in the Farm Forums of Mendenhall Valley and to preparation for her teaching at the Juneau Community College. For 10 years. Mathilda worked enthusiastically as leader of the 4-H Mendenhall Boys Club. 1950-1960. for which she will long be remembered by the young boys. now grown to men. and by their parents for the wonderful inspiration and training she gave them in the various 4-H Club farm programs.

Mathilda Kendler continues to be an inspiration to the men and women of the community, and to her two grandchildren in Juneau, who are the third generation Alaskans. and as such are putting roots and more people in the state who look upon Alaska as a place to put down roots.

Reprinted with permission from the Daily Alaska Empire, *February 8, 1962.*

Mr. and Mrs. Joe Kendler, Sr., of the Glacier Valley highway, will be leaving Juneau soon to make their home in the Seattle area.

Mrs. Kendler was leader to the first continuing 4-H club in southeastern Alaska. Mr. Kendler was ever her able assistant and helper. This boys' club learned much, and won many 4th of July parade and 4-H State honors. Part of their prize money was used recently to purchase a very fine record player for use of all 4-H clubs in the Juneau area.

Coming to Juneau more than 40 years ago as German emigrants, they met on board ship crossing the Atlantic ocean. Through the years - and many obstacles - they cleared land in the Glacier valley area, produced grade-A milk for the Juneau market, but found time to test various vegetable seed and growing methods for the Extension Service and Experiment stations in Alaska.

Always active in Alaska Homemakers, Mrs. Kendler is a member of the Mendenhall Homemakers' Club. A former Extension Service agent influenced Mrs. Kendler to attend clothing classes at the University of Alaska. With her great talent for doing things well, and her great enthusiasm, Mrs. Kendler became a teacher of clothing for the Juneau Community College. In addition, she has assisted numerous women, and especially 4-H girls, with clothing construction.

Our community will miss the Kendlers, but we wish them the best of everything in their new life in the Seattle area.

Courtesy of the author

We were met at the Seattle airport by our daughter Mildred, her husband Dale and their three children. After a few days in their pretty home, we decided to look around for a new house with no more than five rooms, a birch kitchen, and a small yard. After a few weeks of traveling around with real estate salesmen, we finally became convinced that all new houses are enormous with large front and back yards that would need more care than we wanted.

Having just sold our nine-room home with its large, landscaped yard, we finally decided to buy a lot and build a place. But one of the salesmen warned us that a small house like that would never sell. "This day and age, people want large, spacious homes only."

Oh, my, I thought. What do do? Rent an apartment? Joe said no to that. Then one evening when I felt tired and weary from traveling around and looking, I said hesitantly, "How about a mobile home?"

"That would suit me just fine," Joe replied with a sparkle in his warm, brown eyes. So that's how we came to buy a mobile home, and it proved a happy solution for us both. Our double-wide mobile home came with all the modern conveniences, including a fireplace. In addition to a large patio, there was just enough garden space to be enjoyable. Joe helped me plant the rose garden. He

Retired Dairyman And Wife Market Spuds And Eggs In S. E. Alaska

Tons of potatoes and hundreds of chickens fill the barn on the Kendler farm on Glacier highway—a barn that was empty after Joe Kendler retired from the dairy business about two years ago.

Though Joe Kendler's potato growing project was started as a hobby to occupy the retired dairyman—unaccustomed to having time on his hands—the hobby has developed into the only commercial potato growing business in southeast Alaska.

It was a year ago last May that the former dairyman started raising potatoes just to have something to do, and his first crop was such a huge success that this year he really went into the potato raising business in a big way.

His potato raising hobby works well with Mrs. Kendler's hobby of raising laying hens and selling eggs locally.

But to get back to the potatoes— This year's crop of Kendler's potatoes totaled 35 tons or 70,000 pounds—that sounds larger and it is easier to visualize potatoes by the pound than the ton.

SEVEN ACRES OF POTATOES

Kendler sowed about seven acres of ground with certified Netted Gem seed early in May. He did the planting himself with the aid of a Farm-All tractor. The crop was ready for harvesting in October and that job was completed by Mr. and Mrs. Kendler and nine or ten men they hired through the local employment office. An International Automatic Potato Digger did much of the work—and Mrs. Kendler was timekeeper.

A third of the crop has already been sold, but the rest of the potatoes almost fill the 70-foot storage bin down the middle of the former cow barn. Here a thermostatically operated heating unit keeps the barn at the proper temperature for storage of the potatoes.

Potatoes from the Kendler farm have been shipped to markets and individuals in Skagway, Sitka, Hoonah and Pelican and fill standing orders for local stores.

Culls weren't harvested but were left in the ground as fertilizer and are used by Mrs. Kendler for her chickens—which gets us back to the second hobby that is engaging the Kendler family.

CHICKENS A HOBBY, TOO

Mrs. Kendler didn't need another hobby to keep her busy, because she is an active clubwoman—in Toastmistress, Juneau Woman's club, and Homemakers club—the guiding light of the local 4-H clubs and she is a weaving enthusiast, too.

When the 300 baby chicks arrived by Pan American last spring, the laying-hen business probably seemed a little remote. However, the chicks grew like crazy and when they were just 4½ months old on August 15, they started to lay.

That was a record, according to Mrs. Kendler who quotes Clyde G. Sherman of Fairbanks, until recently territorial Commissioner of Agriculture. "Four - and - a - half months old and they are laying? Mr. Sherman could hardly believe it," Mrs. Kendler said of her Parmenter Reds.

EVERYTHING AUTOMATIC

Space in the barn on each side of the large potato bin is utilized for the chickens. Here automatic laying nests have been installed in the poultry units of the barn.

Entrances to the nests can't be seen in the picture—they are away from the camera—but the idea is that as soon as an egg is laid, the egg rolls into an air-cooled compartment where it is kept clear and free from breakage until eggs are gathered for the market.

Pity the poor hen with a motherly instinct who might want to sit on her eggs. She hasn't a chance to raise a family!

Production of the 300 hens averages about 69 per cent and Mrs. Kendler wishes that she had twice as many to fill the orders of the local stores—the California and Home Grocery—that handle her eggs.

Not only are the nests automatic —the poultry units are equipped with automatic feeders that require filling only twice a month and automatic waterers.

The Kendlers, making use of their former dairy land, last year raised oats sufficient for a year's need for feed and bedding for the hens.

And the potato culls—Mrs. Kendler thinks they provide the extra vitamins that keep the chickens extra healthy.

So, with both of the Kendlers starting their enterprises as a hobby, to keep themselves busy, to make use of the farm land and

equipment—they have found themselves with full-sized commercial businesses on their hands.

FAMILY GROWN

To add to their idleness—their children had grown and left home. Joe, Jr., a pilot with Alaska Coastal Airlines, and his wife, the former Betty Bonnett, live in Douglas. Debby, their daughter, is in the picture above. Mildred Kendler, who attended the University of Alaska is now Mrs. Dale Steen, the mother of two children, and lives in Seattle.

Now, between their potatoes and chickens, there is nothing idle about the Kendlers.

"But it isn't work—all of the new automatic equipment makes tending chickens a pleasure instead of a chore," Mrs. Kendler says.

We don't know what Mr. Kendler thinks about all of those potatoes, but he has a smile on his face in the picture.

Reprinted with permission from the Daily Alaska Empire, November 17, 1953.

Teacher's Certificate *Dec 17, 1959*
To Sewing Instructor

A vocational teacher's certificate from the Department of Education issued recently to Mrs. Joe Kendler came to her as an overwhelming surprise.

"I am deeply grateful for so delightful a development," said the well-known local woman, who with her husband devoted over 35 years operating their Alaska dairy farm here on Glacier Highway. Shortly before that she emigrated from her former home in Germany. It is only since the couple retired from, their dairy business a few years ago that Mrs. Kendler took up dressmaking as a hobby —

"Just to have something to do," she states. She never dreamed of ever teaching the subject to others. Yet, just a few months ago Mrs. Kendler was engaged by the Community College here to teach a course in basic sewing, one that was completed "most successfully," she states. Starting sometime in February she will teach two more courses, one in intermediate sewing, and one in tailoring which includes making a suit, according to Dr. Dorothy Novotney, Director of the Community College.

Her progress in sewing Mrs. Kendler credits entirely the local extension service from whose agents she took every one of their very excellent courses. For several years Mrs. Kendler served as sewing project leader for the Mendenhall Homemakers Club, and two years ago she attended a course in the Bishop method of tailoring held at the University of Alaska.

Reprinted with permission from the Daily Alaska Empire, *December 17, 1959.*

particularly loved the sweet perfume of our 18 hybrid rose bushes and climbers that the warm summer breeze swept through our open patio door and windows.

After a couple of years of our serene life and pleasant surroundings, my good husband suddenly passed away. Forty-six congenial years with Joe and then — utter desolation, loneliness. I couldn't fill my days. They were endless.

A few months after Joe's death, a Juneau friend spent the day with me. Jenny knew of my previous interest in fashion work, having been one of my students when I taught dressmaking and tailoring at the Juneau Community College after our retirement from the dairy business in 1953. Looking for work then had been the least of my interests, because we still had a lot to do on the farm. I still remember the day when I answered the telephone and a woman's voice said:

"This is Dorothy Novotney, director of the Juneau Community College. How would you like to take over our dressmaking and tailoring classes?"

Dumbfounded, I couldn't answer! How could they make such a mistake as to ask me? I had no academic training. How could I become a teacher? Something is wrong, I kept thinking.

Dr. Novotney must have sensed my predicament.

"Don't answer immediately," she said. "You can tell me in a couple of days. I know you can do it. I've seen some beautiful garments you've made for your daughter-in-law, Betty."

I promised to call back.

As soon as I hung up the receiver, I dashed over to see a friend of mine who didn't live too far from me. When Gladys heard my story, she urged, "Take it. You have no reason to hesitate. I know you can do it. Besides, those people have heard about the successes you've had all these years with your 4-H members. All those awards! That shows you can teach." She also said, "With your background you'll become a vocational teacher easily."

"One moment I feel flattered, and the next I'm scared to death," I told Gladys, still overwhelmed by Dr. Novotney's phone call.

All at once I remembered the two summer courses I took at the University of Alaska. There the teacher, who taught the Bishop technique in dressmaking and tailoring, had been trained by Mrs. Edna Bryte Bishop herself. Maybe that would qualify me.

My family on Easter Day, 1982, at my mobile home in Alderwood Manor.
Front row from left: Jennifer Smeby; Michelle Smeby; Joseph Smeby; and
Corey Baxter; Scott Baxter is standing just behind Michelle and Joseph.
Middle row: Scott Spickler; Sandy Spickler holding their son, Kyle; Kathleen Lucas;
me; Debbie Baxter; Betty Kendler; Trudy and Matthew Smeby; and Heidi Steen.
In the back from left: Mildred Steen; Dale Steen; Ted Steen; Ron Baxter;
Joe Kendler, Jr.; and George Smeby.

The next day I phoned Dr. Novotney to accept.

"Good," she said. "Now we'll advertise at once. Next Monday will be your first day."

That was the beginning of six happy years of teaching. I was very sorry to have to give it up when we left Juneau.

While Jenny and I finished our lunch, she brought me up to date on Juneau. She had sensed my sorrow, my emptiness since Joe's death.

"You've got to keep busy. Anybody just off the farm can't just sit and pick roses." She told me about a Mr. Roby in south Seattle, a knitting machine importer.

"Why don't you look into that?" she urged me.

A phone call to him got me into contact with the most delightful teacher, Liz Hunt, who lives in our city. Not only did she turn out to be a whiz at her machine, but she also was a most capable teacher.

She and her other students helped me over that depressed and unhappy period. She holds seminars occasionally, and holds monthly open house where we knitters meet and exchange fashion ideas. I bought a machine and soon exchanged it for a more advanced automatic machine with computer and radar attachment. I have become a happy, knit-fashion creator.

Now I remember every one of my family on their birthdays with knitted garments.

This past Christmas alone I completed 16 garments of various sizes and styles: Ski sweaters with Norwegian designs, turtleneck sweaters, plain and fancy, tennis sweaters with knit-in borders of red and blue, several after-five blouses with wide, lacy sleeves, and dresses for wee ones.

Watching my family's pleasure as they unwrap their gifts gives me immense happiness. Their ecstatic *ahs* and *ohs* show appreciation of the work I've performed with my own hands and heart. Through them I've regained my happiness.

———————

Now nearly 80, Mathilde Kendler is still as active and busy as she was before she retired. She visits her many friends, entertains her family in her gracious mobile home, stays in close contact with her friends in Alaska, and knits and knits and knits some more.

And, as in those days when she was feeding her family and the hired hands on the dairy farm, she indulges in her love for cooking whenever the opportunity presents itself. One evening she invited me to dinner and served pork chops surrounded by home-grown carrots, boiled new potatoes, potato pancakes, a zucchini-onion side dish, a tomato-onion side dish, blueberry muffins with homemade strawberry jam, a bean salad, a green salad and cherry chiffon pie with whipped cream for dessert — and that was just for the two of us!

Thank you, Mathilde — for dinner and for sharing your story with us. You are a remarkable person.

Thanks, too, to R.N. De Armond of Juneau for providing the historical notes from the Alaska Daily Empire. *Your research is appreciated.*

—Margy Kotick, Editor

*Joe and me relaxing in our driveway,
summer, 1963. Two years later
we moved to Washington.*

Joe Jr. and Betty, 1982.

*Mildred and Joe Jr. just
before he entered the Army.*

Mildred and Dale Steen, 1980.

*Joe and our granddaughter Sandy,
flying to Seattle, 1960.*

*Joe and me with our oldest
granddaughter, Trudy.*

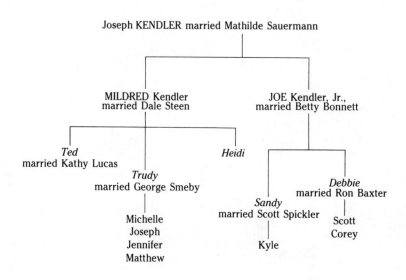

Joseph KENDLER married Mathilde Sauermann

MILDRED Kendler
married Dale Steen

JOE Kendler, Jr.,
married Betty Bonnett

Ted
married Kathy Lucas

Heidi

Trudy
married George Smeby

Sandy
married Scott Spickler

Debbie
married Ron Baxter

Michelle
Joseph
Jennifer
Matthew

Kyle

Scott
Corey